AMBER R. KINLAW

Bologna Travel Guide 2024

Discover Italy's Culinary Delights, Historic Architecture, and Vibrant Culture with an itinerary idea.

First edition

This book was professionally typeset on Reedsy.
Find out more at reedsy.com

Contents

Introduction to Bologna   1

   Bologna's Rich History and Culture   3

Why Visit Bologna   6

Planning Your Trip   8

   Bologna Time Zone   8

   Bologna Visa and Entry Requirements   9

   Best Time to Visit Bologna   10

   Duration of stay recommendations   12

   Creating an Itinerary   14

   Packing List   16

   Budgeting for Your Trip   17

Getting to Bologna   20

   Arriving by Air   21

   Arriving by Bus or Car   22

   Transportation in Bologna   24

   Buses   24

   Trams   24

   Funicular   24

   Urban Bikes   24

   How to Navigate the City Center   25

   Accommodation Options   26

   Hotels and Resorts   27

   Bed and Breakfasts   28

   Hostels and Budget Stays   28

   Apartments and Vacation Rentals   30

Top Tourist Attractions   33

Piazza Maggiore: Bologna's Heart   34

The Two Towers: Asinelli and Garisenda   35

Basilica di San Petronio   37

Archiginnasio of Bologna   38

Neptune's Fountain   40

Bologna's Porticoes   41

Museums and Galleries   44

National Gallery of Bologna   45

MAMbo - Museum of Modern Art   46

Archaeological Museum   48

Museo Ducati   49

Museum of the History of Bologna   51

Exploring Bologna's Art Scene   53

Street Art   53

Contemporary Art Galleries   54

Culinary Delights   55

Bolognese Cuisine: A Culinary Journey   56

Traditional Dishes and Local Specialties   58

Where to Enjoy the Best Pasta in Bologna   59

Exploring the Mercato di Mezzo   59

Wine and Food Tours   61

Cooking Classes and Food Experiences   62

Day Trips and Nearby Attractions   64

Modena: The Land of Balsamic Vinegar   64

Parma: A Gourmet's Paradise   65

Ravenna: Mosaics and Byzantine Treasures   67

Ferrara: A Renaissance Gem   68

Outdoor Adventures in the Apennines   70

Vineyard Tours in the Emilia-Romagna Region   71

Shopping and Souvenir   73

Bologna's Shopping Districts   74

Local Markets and Artisan Shops   75

Fashion and Design Boutiques   77

Souvenirs to Bring Home   78
Entertainment and Nightlife   80
   Theaters and Live Performances   81
   Music Venues and Concerts   82
   Bologna's Thriving Nightlife Scene   84
   Bars and Pubs for Every Taste   85
Cultural Events and Festivals   88
   Other celebrations and events   89
Language and Communication   92
   Language   92
   Communication in Bologna   93
   Basic Italian Phrases   94
Currency and Banking   97
Practical Tips and Safety   99
   Safety Tips for Travelers   99
Health and Medical Services   101
Local Customs and Etiquette   103
Conclusion   105

Introduction to Bologna

Greetings from Bologna: A Journey into the Soul of Italy

Bologna, which is located in the center of Emilia-Romagna, is a shining example of Italian history, culture, and cuisine. This vivacious city, also known as "La Dotta, La Grassa, La Rossa" (The Learned, The Fat, The Red), welcomes guests to immerse themselves in its rich history, mouthwatering food, and loving acceptance of tradition. I'm thrilled to be your tour guide on this excursion into the heart of Bologna since I've had the opportunity to stroll through its charming streets and sample its cuisine.

Bologna's intellectual air cannot be avoided while visiting the city. Bologna has gained its reputation as "The Learned" because of its esteemed university, which was founded in 1088. You'll be surrounded by elaborate archways, enormous libraries, and the animated conversation of students from all over the world as you stroll through the old university area. I couldn't help but feel a kinship with the innumerable intellectuals who had gone before me as I strolled through these neighborhoods.

Of course, a trip to Bologna wouldn't be complete without sampling some of its world-famous cuisine. Bologna, often known as "The Fat," is quite proud of its cuisine. The city is a food lover's heaven, providing a mouthwatering variety of choices, from the region's signature delicious mortadella to the world-famous Bolognese sauce (ragù) that tops fresh tagliatelle pasta. I can still taste the pure joy of enjoying a dish of freshly prepared tortellini at a

1

charming trattoria hidden down a narrow cobblestone path. Every mouthful seemed like a celebration of the skilled culinary tradition.

The urban design and architecture of Bologna are evidence of its historical importance. Due to its terracotta roofs and buildings, the city is known as "The Red" and has a hospitable atmosphere. The complex Basilica of San Petronio and the well-known Neptune Fountain are both located in the bustling center area, Piazza Maggiore. The buildings seem to glow with a flaming color as the sun sets, creating a lovely and unique ambiance.

Bologna's greatest attraction rests in its people and their steadfast ties to their heritage, not only in its sites and cuisine. I had the opportunity of conversing with locals while I was seeing the city, and they were always ready to tell me about their family customs, festivals, and the pride they have in their city's past. It's simple to feel like you've joined a larger group throughout your stay here because of the strong feeling of community that exists here.

Bologna's spirit pours into your soul whether you're strolling through the buzzing Mercato di Mezzo, cycling through the kilometers of porticoes, or just drinking an espresso in a bustling plaza. A timeless and fully modern experience is created by the fusion of history, culture, and culinary genius.

I urge you to let Bologna work its magic on you as you go off on your own trip here. Enjoy every mouthful, embrace the slower pace, and let the tales carved into each brick and cobblestone charm you. Whatever your interests—art, gastronomy, or history—Bologna guarantees a memorable trip that will stay with you long after you've left its alluring embrace. Welcome to Bologna, where the past and present converge to form a unique tapestry of Italian character.

Bologna's Rich History and Culture

Bologna, which is located in the center of Italy, is a vibrant city rich in culture and history that enchants visitors with its many facets. With Etruscan origins, Bologna's illustrious past is evident in every cobblestone street, stately palace, and bustling square. Entering this city is like entering a living museum where the past and current coexist together.

The city's extensive network of porticoes is one of its most recognizable characteristics. These covered walkways, which span a distance of more than 38 kilometers, not only provide useful protection from the weather but also serve as a showcase for Bologna's distinctive architectural style. Asinelli and Garisenda, the city's two most well-known towers, are symbols of its medieval heritage and provide panoramic vistas as compensation for the adventurous traveler's ascent.

Walking through the old town, Piazza Maggiore stands out as the focus of Bologna's cultural life. The plaza, which is surrounded by magnificent structures like the majestic Basilica di San Petronio, is a gathering place for both residents and tourists. Inviting visitors to have a leisurely coffee while admiring the magnificence of the surroundings, cafés overflow into the Piazza.

No trip to Bologna would be complete without indulging in some of the city's delectable cuisine, which is famed for its dynamic environment. The popular Bolognese sauce is said to have originated in this city, and trattorias serve up genuine versions of this well-known meal. Food lovers will find all they need at the Quadrilatero, a lively market area that sells everything from fresh fruit to artisanal cheeses and cured meats. Enrolling in a cooking class offers insight into the techniques used to create classic Italian cuisine for an authentic experience.

Bologna has a wide variety of museums and galleries that will captivate culture buffs. The impressive anatomical theater in the Archiginnasio, once the

3

location of the city's university, attests to Bologna's longstanding significance in the field of education. The modern Italian art on display at the Museo d'Arte Moderna di Bologna (MAMbo) stands in sharp contrast to the city's historic foundations.

As the location of the oldest university in the world, Bologna has a rich intellectual heritage that is closely entwined with its past. The University of Bologna, which was established in 1088, has produced many luminaries, including Nicolaus Copernicus and Dante Alighieri. The old university buildings provide visitors with a sense of the city's long-standing intellectual culture.

As the sun goes down, Bologna's nightlife begins to take on a character of its own. Students and residents gather in osterias and enotecas to share tales, laughs, and glasses of wine made in the area, bringing the streets to life. Every turn in Bologna seems like an invitation to participate in the celebrations because of the city's welcoming and social environment, which lasts far into the wee hours.

The history and culture of Bologna are intertwined throughout, giving visitors a fully immersed experience. Bologna offers a rich tapestry of experiences, from indulging in gastronomic pleasures to taking in architectural marvels to immersing oneself in the city's intellectual past. This Italian treasure has a way of forging a bond that transcends time and location among people who wander its streets.

Bologna's festivals and events provide a dynamic and engaging opportunity to engage with the city's lively atmosphere in addition to its architectural wonders and cultural riches. The "Festa di San Petronio," which honors the city's patron saint, is among the most eagerly awaited occasions. Processions, performances, and a strong feeling of community are all part of this vibrant event, which brings the community together to celebrate their past.

The Bologna Festival's wide roster of classical, jazz, and contemporary acts appeals to music lovers. The world-class performances held in the city's ancient sites, such as Teatro Comunale di Bologna, enable guests to enjoy music in historically significant settings.

Bologna's street art culture will enthrall art enthusiasts. The city has a significant collection of classical art, but it also has a vibrant modern art scene. Numerous walls are covered with vivid and thought-provoking murals and graffiti, giving the urban environment fresh life. Discovering beautiful works of art hidden in unexpected places enhances the traveler's experience.

The fashion scene in Bologna also reflects the city's distinctive fusion of history and contemporary culture. The city, which is well-known for its independent shops and creative studios, has a variety of shopping opportunities to suit both conventional and cutting-edge preferences. Via dell'Indipendenza, a popular shopping district attracts fashion fans with its combination of upscale brands and regional handcrafted goods.

Experiencing the Emilia-Romagna area beyond the city boundaries shows its attractions. Some of Italy's best wines, including Lambrusco and Sangiovese, are produced among the vineyards that dot the gently sloping hills of the region. Exploring these vineyards gives visitors the chance to sample some of the region's outstanding wines as well as get a peek at its rich agricultural history.

Bologna's appeal extends beyond just sightseeing; it also involves enjoying the pace of daily living. Getting to know the inhabitants, whether via chit-chat at a café or involvement in community activities, provides a window into the character of the city. Every visitor is made to feel like a valued guest by the warmth and friendliness of the Bolognese people, who are fundamental to the essence of the city.

Why Visit Bologna

Bologna, the intriguing regional capital of Emilia-Romagna in northern Italy, is a hidden treasure that awaits exploration by tourists looking for a genuine and educational experience. This dynamic city skillfully combines history, art, gastronomy, and a thriving local culture, making it an alluring destination for tourists of all kinds. I'm here to give my practical insights on why Bologna should be on your must-see travel list after having just recently visited this enchanting city.

Delicious Food: A Gastronomic Paradise

Bologna's culinary scene is renowned and is referred to as "La Grassa" or "The Fat One" for its exceptional food selections. Popular Italian delicacies like tortellini, tagliatelle al ragù (Bolognese sauce), and mortadella were created in this city. Wander around its vibrant markets, such as Mercato delle Erbe or Quadrilatero, to get a taste of the local wines, cured meats, fresh fruit, and cheeses. You may experience the true tastes of Italy by exploring these marketplaces, which is a sensory trip.

Architectural and Historical Wonders

The streets of Bologna are interlaced with the city's rich history. The city has a charming, well-preserved medieval core that may be found everywhere. The Basilica di San Petronio and the Palazzo d'Accursio, two imposing architectural masterpieces, surround Piazza Maggiore, the city's central plaza. Torre degli

Asinelli and Torre Garisenda, the city's two most recognizable towers, provide a window into its medieval history and a breathtaking panoramic view of the city from the summit.

Increased student culture

Bologna's thriving student community gives the city a youthful feel. The University of Bologna, one of the oldest institutions in the world, is located in this vibrant city, which hosts a wide range of cultural events, art exhibits, and music festivals. The city's student population keeps it lively and always changing, resulting in a distinctive fusion of heritage and contemporary.

Museums and Art everywhere

When visiting Bologna, art lovers will be in their element. Giotto, Raffaello, and Tintoretto are just a few of the famous Italian painters whose paintings may be seen at the Pinacoteca Nazionale di Bologna. The Anatomical Theatre and a beautiful library with elaborate wood carvings may be found in the Archiginnasio, a former university building. The museums and galleries of Bologna provide an incredible voyage through Italy's cultural legacy.

Access Point to the Area

Due to its advantageous position, Bologna is a great base for exploring the greater Emilia-Romagna area. Day tours from Bologna may take you everywhere, including the enchanted town of Ravenna, which is renowned for its magnificent mosaics, and the opulent motorcar mecca of Modena, where you can visit the Ferrari Museum. The lovely scenery, famous wines, and ancient villages of the area are all easily accessible

Planning Your Trip

Making a trip to Bologna requires careful planning. The first step is to plan your vacation so that you may see Bologna's beauty at its most authentic without the hectic masses. The calm spring and the enthralling autumn are the best times to go exploring.

Consider allocating 3 to 4 days to this Italian gem when choosing the length of your visit. A period of this length enables thorough exploration of historical marvels and cultural riches. Making a thorough plan reveals a symphony of experiences, from seeing lively piazzas to climbing recognizable structures.

Remember to bring suitable shoes for walking around cobblestone streets, weather-appropriate clothing, and things to take pictures of in this gorgeous setting. To get the most out of your trip, set aside a decent amount of money for lodging, food, and local transportation.

Bologna Time Zone

Bologna, Italy is in the Central European Time (CET) zone, which runs from UTC+1 in the winter to UTC+2 in the summer. This implies that during the winter, Bologna is one hour ahead of Coordinated Universal Time (UTC) and two hours ahead of UTC during the summer.

When CET is UTC+1 in the winter, the time difference between Bologna and PST is 8 hours. For example, 12:00 PM in Bologna corresponds to 4:00 AM in

PST.

The time difference between Bologna and PST is 7 hours during the summer, when CET is UTC+2. For example, 12:00 PM in Bologna corresponds to 5:00 AM in PST.

Bologna's time zone changes twice a year, between March and October. The clocks move forward one hour on the final Sunday of March to commence Daylight Saving Time (DST). The clocks are set back one hour on the final Sunday of October to mark the conclusion of Daylight Saving Time.

Bologna Visa and Entry Requirements

Bologna visa requirements:

Most foreign nationals need a visa to enter Italy. To find out whether you require a visa, contact your nearest Italian embassy or consulate.

Because the visa application procedure might take several weeks, it is critical to apply as soon as possible.

A passport, visa application form, and other papers will be required.

The following are the visa application costs for nationals of certain countries:

- United States: €80
- United Kingdom: €80
- Canada: €80
- Australia: €80
- New Zealand: €80
- China: €116
- India: €116
- Brazil: €116

- Russia: €116
- South Africa: €80

Entry requirements for Bologna:

- You must have a valid passport to enter Italy.
- Your passport must be valid for at least three months after your planned departure date from Italy.
- It is also necessary to have a return or onward ticket
- You may also be required to produce evidence of adequate means to maintain yourself while in Italy.

Other admission criteria include:

You may also be required to provide evidence of immunization for certain illnesses, such as yellow fever.

The specific criteria differ depending on your nationality, so check with your nearest Italian embassy or consulate

Exemptions from visa requirements

Some nations' citizens are excluded from the visa requirement for Italy.

The European Union, Switzerland, Norway, Iceland, Liechtenstein, and San Marino are among these nations.

Best Time to Visit Bologna

Bologna's weather, events, and visitor crowds change throughout the year, so picking the ideal time to come may have a big impact on how you feel about the city.

Spring (March to May):

Because of Bologna's temperate temperatures and flower landscapes, spring is one of the greatest seasons to visit. Bologna gradually warms up in March as winter slips away, which is perfect for seeing the city's outdoor attractions like Piazza Maggiore and the Two Towers without the summer heat. With brilliant blooms and blooming trees, the lovely parks, including Giardini Margherita, come to life and provide a pleasant setting for strolls.

Bologna experiences its genuine spring in April and May when the days are nice and the evenings are chilly. The Fiera di San Luca, a centuries-old celebration that combines history with current entertainment, is a classic festival that is best experienced around this time of year. Remember that spring is also the shoulder season, so there will be fewer visitors around than during the busiest summer months.

Summer (June to August):

Bologna's summers are pleasant and welcoming, making them a great time to visit if you want a livelier environment. The peak tourist season, which begins in June, has longer days and a packed roster of activities. However, due to the influx of tourists from all over the globe who come to Bologna to enjoy its famous culinary scene, ancient architecture, and rich culture, the city can become rather busy, particularly in July and August.

Bologna showcases its artistic side throughout the summer by holding several festivals, concerts, and open-air film screenings. Although July may see the highest temperatures, the many gelato shops and cool streets provide a reprieve from the heat. Summer can be the greatest season to come if you don't mind enormous crowds and want to take part in a joyful mood.

Autumn (September to November):

As a lovely and more sedate alternative to the busy summer months, autumn provides. With sunny days and mild nights, September is very pleasant and offers a favorable environment for exploring. Less popular historical buildings in the city, such as the Basilica di San Petronio and the Archiginnasio, let you take your time learning about the history and architecture of the area.

Autumn in Bologna is one of the best times to visit because of the vibrant array of hues that cover the hills and vineyards around. This time of year is ideal for day travels to adjacent rural areas and wine-tasting excursions at famous Emilia-Romagna wineries. Fall is a season of culinary plenty as well, with truffle festivals and food markets showcasing the area's top-notch cuisine.

Winter (December to February):

Despite being the off-peak season, Bologna still has something special to offer those who don't mind the chilly weather. The city is lively in December as Christmas markets and other decorations line the streets. With an amazing Christmas tree and an ice skating rink, the main Piazza Maggiore is transformed into a winter paradise.

The coldest months, January and February, provide a more sedate and private setting for seeing indoor sites like museums and art galleries. During the winter months, the famed food of Bologna, which features substantial meals like tortellini in brodo, is especially soothing. The Teatro Comunale di Bologna also has a robust schedule of operatic performances throughout the winter months if you're a fan.

Duration of stay recommendations

It's important to take into account the ideal amount of time to spend in Bologna while making travel plans so that you can fully experience the city's rich history, lively culture, and delectable cuisine. Even while the city may not be as huge as other of Italy's bigger metropolises, the variety of experiences it offers calls for careful consideration of how much time to provide for each.

Two to three days is the perfect length of time for a quick yet enjoyable vacation. You may take use of this time to discover the city's top attractions and experience its distinct charm. The Piazza Maggiore, the center of Bologna, where the Basilica di San Petronio and the Palazzo Comunale are located, is a great place to start your tour. The nearby Quadrilatero Market neighborhood entices with its winding lanes and offers a variety of food vendors, artisan stores, and regional goods to relish.

However, extending your trip to 4 or 5 days is advised if you want to learn more about Bologna's culture and history. This time frame permits a slower pace, allowing you to discover lesser-known gems. Visit the Sanctuary of the Madonna di San Luca in the hills beyond the city; it is reachable by the well-known Portico di San Luca, a covered walkway with 666 arches.

Visits to the Archaeological Museum and the Museum of Modern Art of Bologna (MAMbo) are worthwhile for museum fans. Art enthusiasts shouldn't pass up the chance to see pieces by well-known Bolognese painters including the Carracci family and Guido Reni. Visiting the Museo Enzo Ferrari and learning about the origins of balsamic vinegar may also be made more enriching by taking a day trip to the adjacent town of Modena.

Consider extending your stay to a week if seeing Bologna's food scene on its whole is important to you. You can appreciate the city's status as Italy's gastronomic center at this time. In addition to delighting in pasta delicacies like tortellini and tagliatelle al ragù (Bolognese sauce), you can sign up for culinary workshops to master the tricks of age-old recipes.

A longer stay also gives visitors the chance to take advantage of the city's busy event schedule. You may interact more deeply with Bologna's vibrant cultural scene if your trip falls on occasions like the Cinema Ritrovato festival or the Arte Fiera contemporary art show.

Creating an Itinerary

It takes a careful balancing of historical allure, culinary pleasures, and vivid cultural activities to create an interesting and thorough itinerary for a tourist experiencing Bologna. Bologna, an Italian city in the Emilia-Romagna region, has a wide variety of attractions that appeal to history buffs, foodies, and art lovers alike.

Day 1: Historical Marvels and Artistic Gems

Immerse yourself in Bologna's past before setting off on your tour. Start your day by going to the city's central Piazza Maggiore, which is bordered by ancient structures including the Basilica di San Petronio and the Palazzo dei Notai. Admire the Neptune Fountain and the exquisite Gothic architecture.

Visit the Archiginnasio, a former university building with beautiful wood-carved ornamentation, to further explore Bologna's creative past. Wander through its historic library, which is filled with a treasure trove of rare volumes and manuscripts, and explore its anatomical theater.

Day 2: Culinary Exploration

The culinary scene of Bologna is well known, especially for its pasta dishes. Start your day by taking a trip around the bustling Quadrilatero Market, a tangle of vendors selling local specialties, fresh fruit, cheeses, and meats. Try local specialties like mortadella and Parmigiano-Reggiano cheese while interacting with the community.

Tagliatelle al ragù, the city's iconic pastas dish, may be enjoyed at a trattoria for lunch. Indulge in a traditional Bolognese dinner there. After that, enroll in a culinary class to learn how to make fresh pasta from scratch.

Day 3: Towers and Views

Explore Bologna's stunning skyline by going on a tower-hopping journey. Start with the Asinelli and Garisenda Towers, two medieval buildings that tilt and provide sweeping views of the city. For a breathtaking viewing point, ascend the Asinelli Tower.

Visit the Museo Civico Medievale, which has a magnificent collection of historical objects and works of literature, thereafter. Through its historical exhibits, explore the city's rich history.

Day 4: Culture and the Arts

Spend the day discovering Bologna's extensive creative legacy. Visit the Pinacoteca Nazionale, the National Gallery of Bologna, which has a magnificent collection of Italian paintings from the 13th to the 18th centuries. Admire the creations of well-known painters like Carracci and Raphael.

Visit the MAMbo (Museo d'Arte Moderna di Bologna) in the afternoon to see modern works of art by Italian and foreign artists. Discover the rich contemporary art culture of the city.

Day 5: Visit Ravenna for the day

Visit Ravenna for the day; it is a UNESCO World Heritage site known for its magnificent Byzantine mosaics. View the exquisite mosaics of biblical subjects at the Basilica of San Vitale. To discover more about the history of the city, visit Dante's Tomb and the Mausoleum of Galla Placidia.

Once you get back to Bologna, take your time dining at one of the city's quaint osterias while tasting regional cuisine and regional wines.

The combination of history, gastronomy, and art in Bologna makes for an amazing vacation. Travelers may immerse themselves in the city's rich past, experience its wonderful cuisines, and discover its artistic treasures by following this carefully selected itinerary, making memories.

Packing List

- Walking shoes that are comfy: Bologna will need a lot of walking, so it's crucial to have comfortable footwear.
- Pack a rain jacket since Bologna sometimes experiences rain.
- Packing sunglasses is a smart idea since Bologna's sun may be rather powerful.
- Hat: It is a good idea to take a hat since Bologna may become quite hot in the sun.
- Camera: Since Bologna is a beautiful city, you should pack a camera to record all of your experiences.
- Sunscreen: Bologna may experience intense sun exposure, thus sunscreen should be brought along.
- Pack insect repellent, as Bologna tends to be a bitchy city.
- Money belt: Using a money belt to carry your cash and passport is secure.
- First-aid kit: In the event of an accident, a first-aid kit might be useful.
- Put your necessities, including toothpaste, a toothbrush, shampoo, and conditioner, in your bag.
- Clothing: Bring layered, comfy clothes. Packing a variety of warm and cold weather attire is an excellent idea since Bologna's weather may change quickly.

Depending on your plans and interests, you may also wish to bring the following items:

- You must bring the proper attire and equipment if you want to go hiking or engage in other outdoor activities.
- You should bring warmer attire, such as a coat, scarf, and gloves if you're traveling in the winter.
- You will need to pack extra goods if you are traveling with kids, such as diapers, wipes, and a stroller.

- Jacket or sweater? Packing a sweater or jacket is an excellent idea since Bologna may become cool in the evenings.
- Swimsuit: Be sure to bring a swimsuit if you want to swim in the sea or a pool.
- Water bottle with insulation: This is a practical method to remain hydrated when traveling.
- Keep your electronic gadgets charged while you are traveling by using a portable charger.
- Travel adapter: If you are departing from a nation with several electrical outlets, be sure to bring one with you.

Budgeting for Your Trip

Creating a Budget for Your Bologna Trip

It may be fun and educational to plan a vacation to the lovely city of Bologna in Italy. It's essential to develop a thorough budget that accounts for every part of your trip if you want to get the most out of your vacation without going over budget. The following is a detailed guide on setting a budget for your trip to Bologna, including everything from lodging and travel to meals and sights.

Accommodation:

In terms of lodging, Bologna has a variety of possibilities to fit various budgets. A cost-effective option is a hostel dormitory, which may range from €20 to €40 per night. Midrange hotels or Airbnb homes costing between €70 and €120 per night may be available if you desire more solitude. Luxury lodgings and high-end hotels may cost more than $150 per night.

Transportation:

There may be a cost for plane travel to go to Bologna, and that cost will depend on where you leave from and the season. The cost of round-trip flights from

European locations may vary from €50 to €300. Consider purchasing a Bologna Welcome Card, which costs €14 and offers 48 hours of unrestricted public transit usage, to get around the city. As an alternative, it is common and costs around €10 per day to hire a bike.

Meals:

Bologna's famed culinary treats must be tasted, although restaurant prices might vary. Local trattorias and pizzerias often charge between €15 and €30 for a meal that includes a main dish and a beverage. Try street cuisine like piadinas (€5–€7) or have a fast dinner from a panini shop (€6–€10) for a more affordable choice. You may also save money by cooking part of your meals using goods from nearby markets (€30 to €50 per week).

Sightseeing:

It is essential to see Bologna's historical landmarks and tourist attractions. Major attractions like the Towers of Bologna have a $5–$10 entrance charge. Entry fees to museums like the Museo Civico Archeologico and the Museo di Palazzo Poggi range from around €10 to €15. Consider a Bologna Card, which costs between €25 and €30 and provides discounts and free access to several locations, if you want to visit several sites.

Entertainment:

Budget-friendly ways to experience Bologna's thriving entertainment scene include going to free events like fairs or markets. A movie ticket for a night out typically costs between €8 and €12, while a beverage at a pub costs between €7 and €10. Depending on the performance, cover rates at live music venues might range from €5 to €20.

Miscellaneous:

Don't forget to include extra spending money and mementos in your budget. It's a good idea to set aside between €50 and €100 for unforeseen expenses. This may be used to pay for items like gratuities, unforeseen transportation costs, and little memento purchases.

Total spending:

A daily budget of between €50 and €70 for lodging, transportation, food, and essential activities is fair for a tourist on a tight budget. While those looking for premium experiences should spend €200 or more per day, mid-range tourists may only have €100 to €150 available.

Getting to Bologna

Traveling to Bologna, Italy provides a plethora of transportation alternatives catered to a variety of interests. Arriving by flight is the best option for people who value speed and distance. Bologna has a well-connected international airport that welcomes visitors from all over the world. If the allure of a picturesque trip appeals to you, consider the enticing alternative of arriving by train. The large train network gives convenience, comfort, and the chance to take in the gorgeous Italian scenery.

The route calls out to the most daring - Arriving by bus or vehicle gives you a feeling of independence, allowing you to explore at your own speed. The roads and streets are well-kept, allowing for a smooth approach to this interesting city. Not to mention public transit inside Bologna, which is a monument to Italy's efficiency. Buses and trams crisscross the city, making monuments and hidden jewels easily accessible.

In this guide for seasoned travelers, we will go through each of these options in depth. Whether you're a seasoned traveler or going on a new trip, this subchapter will provide you with insights into each means of transportation, guaranteeing a seamless and pleasant arrival in Bologna.

Arriving by Air

Travelers have a wonderful chance to see Bologna's intriguing city and its rich history when they fly into the city. Bologna provides guests with a smooth and pleasurable arrival experience with its well-connected airport and practical transportation alternatives. This chapter on what to anticipate while flying into Bologna's airport, getting through customs and immigration, and entering the city center was put together using the knowledge of seasoned visitors.

- **Preparing for Arrival:** It's important to acquire key details regarding your trip, such as the arrival time and terminal, before stepping foot in Bologna. You may use apps and online flight monitors to remain informed about any last-minute changes.
- **Guglielmo Marconi Airport:** Guglielmo Marconi Airport (BLQ), which offers up-to-date amenities and effective services, is the airport that serves Bologna. Because of its small size, the airport is easy to navigate. Due to its closeness to the city's heart, you can get there in a shorter amount of time and enjoy everything that Bologna has to offer.
- **Immigration and Customs** Follow the directions to passport control and customs after disembarking. Passengers from the EU and Schengen often encounter shorter lineups, however, non-EU visitors should budget extra time for possible lines. The procedure moves more quickly if you are prepared with your admission documentation, passport, and visa (if necessary).
- **Baggage Claim:** Guglielmo Marconi Airport's baggage claim is normally quick, but it's a good idea to double-check your luggage's carousel number before getting off the aircraft. There are baggage trolleys available, and porters can help if necessary.
- **Transportation Options:** There are many ways to go from the airport to the city center, A well-liked alternative that offers direct and reasonably priced connectivity is the Aerobus. There are also man taxis accessible, which is a handy but more expensive option. Car rentals are available at

the airport for individuals who would rather do it alone.

- **Navigating Language and Signs:** Although English is frequently spoken in tourist regions, knowing a few basic Italian phrases may help you communicate with people more effectively. Clear and bilingual signage makes it easy to navigate the airport.
- **Money Matters:** While there are a few currency exchange booths at the airport, you could get better deals by using an ATM to get your money. In the whole city, major credit cards are commonly accepted.
- **SIM Cards and Connectivity:** Get a local SIM card at the airport or in the city for a smooth connection. Having access to data and phone choices on these cards enables you to maintain contact when traveling.
- **Airport Services:** Guglielmo Marconi Airport has a range of services, including lounges, retail, restaurants, and Wi-Fi access, in case you arrive early or have a stopover.
- **Exploring Bologna:** Use Bologna's enormous public transit network, which includes buses and trains, after you've arrived in the city. Due to the city's structure favoring pedestrians, cycling, and walking are also common alternatives.

Arriving by Bus or Car

Choosing to arrive in Bologna by bus or car ensures a magical start to this alluring Italian city. The scenery changes from verdant countryside to a wonderful fusion of old-world beauty and contemporary vitality as you get closer to the city boundaries.

If you're traveling by bus, the trip provides a relaxing transit through charming Italian towns. The excitement grows as the bus travels past large vineyards and rolling hills, providing sights of historic castles perched on hilltops. Before arriving in Bologna, the drive offers a unique view of the soft beauty of the surrounding countryside.

The bus travels through busy streets and charming lanes as it approaches the city's center. You can feel Bologna's bustling bustle and see the beautiful porticoes that border the walkways, providing both architectural grandeur and shelter. The old city, with its recognizable terracotta roofs and magnificent towers that punctuate the skyline, comes into view.

The experience is just as intriguing whether you decide on the independence of a road trip in a vehicle. As you drive through quaint villages and along well-kept motorways and scenic routes, you may get glimpses of Italian life. As you see road signs directing you to Bologna, a city renowned for its rich history and gastronomic pleasures, your enthusiasm grows.

When traveling to Bologna by vehicle, you may marvel at the flawless fusion of the past and present. The city's historic walls provide witness to its illustrious past, while the new structures scattered throughout demonstrate its vibrant present. You go through tree-lined boulevards where the variety of architectural designs demonstrates how the city has changed over the years.

As you make your way through Bologna's twisty streets, the excitement grows. You'll be in awe of the porticoes that line practically every street, giving Bologna its distinctive architectural style. As you stroll through the city, these covered walkways provide protection from the weather and a feeling of continuity.

The moment you reach Bologna's medieval center is the pinnacle of your adventure. Finding parking may be difficult if you've ever driven, but once you do, you enter a magical realm. The Piazza Maggiore, the city's beating center, extends a warm welcome. The Basilica di San Petronio stands as a tribute to the city's architectural brilliance and is framed by grand medieval structures.

Getting to Bologna by bus or vehicle provides a sensory extravaganza. Freshly baked bread's scent entices you to visit the nearby bakeries and cafés by wafting through the air. A mellow melody of urban life is created as inhabitants go about their daily business on cobblestone streets.

Transportation in Bologna

Bologna has an extensive public transit network, making it a well-connected metropolis. The bus, which is run by TPER, is the primary form of transportation. A funicular, a few tram lines, and a bike-sharing program are also available.

Buses

There is a robust bus system that travels across the whole city. With an average wait time of 10-15 minutes, buses operate regularly. Newsstands, cigarette stores, and ticket machines all sell tickets. Additionally, a range of cheap tickets, including day passes and weekly passes, are offered.

Trams

Bologna now has three tram lines that go through the heart of the city and some of the nearby neighborhoods. Trams are a speedy alternative to buses for moving about the city's core. The same sites where bus tickets are sold also sell train tickets.

Funicular

The San Luca hill and the city center are connected by a short, steep train known as the funicular. In addition to being a well-liked tourist attraction, it offers a practical route to the hill's summit. Purchase of tickets is possible at the funicular station.

Urban Bikes

BiciBologna is the name of the city's bicycle network. Over 300 docking stations may be found across the city where you can pay to hire a bike. Renting a bike is available for 30, 1, or 24 hours.

How to Navigate the City Center

Bologna's city core is rather compact and tiny, making it simple to navigate on foot or by bicycle. The bus, though, is your best option if you must use public transit. In the middle of the city, at **Piazza XX Settembre**, is where you'll find the main bus terminal.

Accessing the Airport and Leaving It

About 6 kilometers separate the city core from Bologna Airport. Between the airport and the city center, a direct bus route operates. It takes the bus roughly 20 minutes to travel. The bus driver is where you can buy tickets.

Advice for Using Bologna's Public Transportation

- As soon as you get on the bus or tram, validate your ticket.
- Know the many ticket options and choose the one that best meets your requirements.
- Watch the time since certain tickets are only good for a limited amount of time.
- Be kind to your fellow travelers and keep the aisles clear.
- Overall, using public transit to move about Bologna is a practical and economical option.
- With a little preparation, you can simply get everywhere you need to go without having to worry about traffic or parking.

Here are some more tips for using public transit in Bologna:

- Get the TPER app now. This software offers a map of the public transportation system together with real-time information on bus and tram timetables.
- Utilize the Bologna Welcome Card. You may use public transit for free and get discounts on activities and attractions when you use this card.

- If you need assistance, ask. Your demands for public transportation are happily accommodated by the workers at the main bus station and the tourist information centers.

Accommodation Options

Exploring the vibrant city of Bologna provides a range of hotel alternatives to satisfy seasoned tourists as well as newcomers. Hotels and resorts in Bologna provide a variety of options for people seeking exquisite comfort and top-tier services, ranging from boutique lodgings to globally famous brands.

Bed & breakfasts are a beautiful choice if you want a more private and customized experience. These lodgings, located in the city's center or its charming districts, provide a view into local life, as well as full breakfasts to start your day.

Budget travelers will find shelter in the abundance of hostels and low-cost accommodations that dot the landscape of Bologna. These hotels guarantee cost without sacrificing comfort or cleanliness to build a sense of community among like-minded globetrotters.

Apartments and holiday rentals abound for individuals seeking a home-away-from-home experience. These alternatives, which are ideal for families or longer vacations, provide you with the freedom to explore the city while enjoying the luxuries of a fully furnished house.

Bologna also offers unusual lodging options for an out-of-the-ordinary trip. This might be rustic farm stays in the countryside, old castles converted into lodges, or even Eco-friendly getaways for the ecologically aware tourist.

Hotels and Resorts

B&B Hotel Bologna

- Price: From €70 per night
- Amenities include free Wi-Fi, air conditioning, a flat-screen TV, and a private bathroom.
- Location: Zona Artigianale, 5 kilometers from Bologna city center

Hotel NH Bologna Villanova

- Price: From €90 per night
- Amenities include free Wi-Fi, air conditioning, a flat-screen TV, a minibar, and an en suite bathroom.
- Location: Via Villanova, 29/8, 2 kilometers from the heart of Bologna

Suite Hotel Elite

- Price: From €100 per night
- Amenities include free Wi-Fi, air conditioning, a flat-screen TV, a minibar, an en suite bathroom, and a balcony.
- Location: Via Aurelio Saffi 40, 1 mile from the heart of Bologna

4 Star Bologna: Rooms & Apartments

- Price: From €120 per night
- Amenities include free Wi-Fi, air conditioning, a flat-screen TV, a kitchenette, and a private bathroom.
- Location: Viale Angelo Masini, 20 / 22, 3 kilometers from the heart of Bologna

Bed and Breakfasts

Affittacamere di Andrea Bertolino is in San Lazzaro di Savena, a Bologna suburb. It is a modest, family-run bed and breakfast with just four rooms. The rooms are modest yet clean and pleasant, with private bathrooms in each. Breakfast is provided in the dining room and is included in the price. The B&B is roughly a 15-minute drive from downtown, although there is a free shuttle service. The nightly rate begins at €50.

The Bologna Bed & Breakfast is situated in the city center, near the Piazza Maggiore. It is a modest B&B with just five rooms. The rooms are contemporary and attractive, with private bathrooms in each. Breakfast is provided in the breakfast room and is included in the fee. Many of Bologna's attractions are within walking distance of the B&B. The nightly rate begins at €70.

The B&B Hotel Bologna is situated on the outskirts of Bologna in the Zona Artigianale, a business neighborhood. It's a contemporary hotel with bright, roomy rooms. Private bathrooms and flat-screen TVs are standard in all rooms. Breakfast is provided at the buffet restaurant and is included in the fee. There is a free parking lot at the hotel. The nightly rate begins at €60.

The Bed and Breakfast La Piazzetta della Pioggia is situated in the city center, near the University of Bologna. It is a frescoed ceilinged 15th-century palace. The rooms are contemporary and pleasant, with private bathrooms in each. Breakfast is provided in the breakfast room and is included in the fee. Many of Bologna's attractions are within walking distance of the B&B. The nightly rate begins at €80.

Hostels and Budget Stays

Combo Bologna is a well-known hostel in the Navile area, about a 10-minute walk from the city center. It offers a range of dorm and private rooms, as well as a communal kitchen, common area, and laundry room. Prices for a dorm bed start at €25 per night.

Ostello del Sole is a more laid-back hostel in a quiet residential neighborhood within a short walk from the city center. It offers a range of dorm and private rooms, as well as a shared kitchen, a common area, and a garden. A dorm bed costs as little as €22 per night.

Bologna Bed and Breakfast is a bed & breakfast in the heart of the city. There are a few private rooms available, all with en-suite baths. Breakfast is included in the fee, and the hosts are quite kind and helpful. Prices for a private room begin at €50 per night.

The Ghetto is a hotel that was built on the site of a former Jewish ghetto. It is a one-of-a-kind and historic lodging choice in the heart of the city center. Prices for a double room start at €100 per night.

When selecting a budget-friendly hostel or budget stay in Bologna, keep your budget, travel style, and requirements in mind. If you are traveling in a group, you might consider staying in a hostel with shared dorm rooms. If you prefer a more intimate experience, try a bed & breakfast or a low-cost hotel with private rooms.

It is also important to evaluate the location of the hostel or low-cost accommodation. If you want to be at the midst of the activity, you should stay in a hostel or a low-cost hotel in the city center. If you prefer a more relaxing and tranquil stay, consider staying at a hostel or cheap hotel in a quieter neighborhood.

Whatever your budget or travel style, there is a budget-friendly hostel or budget stay in Bologna to suit you. Before making a choice, do some research and weigh your possibilities.

Here are some more suggestions for finding a cheap hostel or somewhere to stay in Bologna:

- Plan ahead of time, particularly if you're going during the high season.
- Look for hostels or low-cost accommodations that provide discounts for extended stays.
- Consider sleeping in a hostel or a low-cost hotel outside of the city core. This will save you money on lodging, but it will also require you to use public transit or walk to the city center.
- Be flexible with your trip dates. If you are willing to be flexible, you may be able to get better prices on lodging.

Apartments and Vacation Rentals

Unique Accommodation Experiences

Nice Apartments in Downtown is an excellent choice for individuals searching for a centrally situated apartment with all the facilities they want. There is a fully equipped kitchen, a washer and dryer, and free WiFi throughout the unit. It's also a short distance from Piazza Maggiore and the Two Towers. A two-bedroom apartment starts at €70 per night.

Hiwya: Apartments for rent in Bologna are another excellent alternative for low-cost apartments in Bologna. The apartments are placed in a variety of areas, so you are sure to find one that meets your requirements. Every apartment has a kitchen, a bathroom, and free WiFi. A one-bedroom apartment starts at €50 per night.

Affitti Brevi Italia Bologna - Case per Vacanze e-Business is a holiday rental firm in Bologna that provides a broad range of flats and residences for rent. The apartments are available in a variety of pricing levels, so you may select one that meets your needs. The agency has examined all of the flats, so you can be certain that they are clean and pleasant. A studio apartment starts at €40 per night.

When looking for a low-cost apartment or vacation rental in Bologna, keep your budget, travel style, and requirements in mind. If you are going to a large party, you should consider renting an apartment with numerous bedrooms. If you prefer a more private experience, try renting a holiday home with its own entrance and terrace.

It is also critical to evaluate the apartment's or vacation rental's location. If you want to be right in the middle of the excitement, you should select an apartment or vacation rental in the city center. If you prefer a more relaxing and tranquil stay, you might opt for an apartment or vacation rental in a quieter area.

Whatever your budget or travel style, there is a budget-friendly apartment or vacation rental in Bologna for you.

Here are some further suggestions for locating a low-cost apartment or holiday rental in Bologna:

- Plan ahead of time, particularly if you're going during the high season.
- Look for apartments or vacation rentals that provide long-term savings.
- Consider staying in a vacation rental or apartment situated outside the city core. This will save you money on lodging, but it will also require you to use public transit or walk to the city center.
- Be flexible with your trip dates. If you are willing to be flexible, you may be able to get better prices on lodging.

I hope this helps you locate the ideal low-cost apartment or vacation rental in Bologna!

Here are some more helpful hints for locating and renting a low-cost apartment or holiday rental in Bologna:

- Use a reputable rental website like Airbnb, Booking.com, or VRBO.
- Read the reviews thoroughly before making a reservation.

- Inquire about any hidden expenses, such as cleaning or security deposits.
- If feasible, try to negotiate the price.

Top Tourist Attractions

A trip to Bologna's city center provides a fascinating tapestry of history and culture, revealing the spirit of this dynamic Italian city. Piazza Maggiore, a vast plaza that pulsates with energy, is at the center of it all. The plaza, surrounded by historic buildings, is a focus of activity where inhabitants and tourists congregate to enjoy the city's vibrant atmosphere.

A short walk from the square brings you to the famed Two Towers, Asinelli and Garisenda, which stand as towering reminders of Bologna's medieval heritage. Their grandeur and leanness are a sight to see, providing panoramic vistas to visitors who mount their ancient stairs.

The majestic Basilica of San Petronio dominates the piazza's landscape. Its grandeur is reflected in a fusion of architectural forms, and its interior has delicate elements that tell the tale of the city's rich past.

The Archiginnasio of Bologna welcomes people interested in academics. Its magnificent anatomical theater and centuries-old inscriptions give respect to the quest for knowledge, which was once the hub of study.

Among the charms of the plaza is Neptune's Fountain, an artistic masterpiece that pays honor to the sea deity. Its elaborate sculptures and grandeur ambiance provide a peaceful setting for reflection.

The city's most distinguishing feature, though, is its elaborate network of

Porticoes. These arching walkways extend for kilometers, giving shade from both the sun and rain. You'll uncover an urban wonder that is both utilitarian and architecturally spectacular when you wander under their charming arcades.

Bologna's city center is intriguing and diversified, inviting guests to immerse themselves in a domain where history, art, and urban life perfectly meet.

Piazza Maggiore: Bologna's Heart

Piazza Maggiore is Bologna's major square in Italy. It is one of Italy's largest and most important squares, and it has been the center of political, social, and cultural activity in Bologna for centuries.

Many notable structures surround the area, including the Basilica di San Petronio, the Palazzo d'Accursio, and the Palazzo del Podestà. It's also a major tourist location, so there's usually something going on.

Here are some of the activities available at Piazza Maggiore:

- Visit the Basilica of San Petronio, Bologna's biggest church. The church is still under construction, but it is a sight to behold.
- Take a stroll around the city's oldest university, the Archiginnasio. The Archiginnasio is now a library, but its exquisite architecture is still worth seeing.
- Visit the city hall, the Palazzo d'Accursio. The Bologna Museum of Modern and Contemporary Art is housed in the Palazzo d'Accursio.
- Enjoy a coffee or a meal at one of the square's many cafés and eateries.
- Walk through the porticoes that border the square.
- The porticoes offer shade and protection from the sun and rain.
- Participate in a performance or festival on the square. The Piazza Maggiore is frequently utilized as a venue for concerts and festivals.

Here are some suggestions for getting about Piazza Maggiore and the city center of Bologna:

- Piazza Maggiore is best visited in the morning or early evening, when it is less busy.
- If you want to understand more about the square's history, you may join a guided tour.
- There are several cafés and restaurants on the plaza, so you will have no trouble finding something to eat or drink.
- If you plan on attending a performance or event in the plaza, get there early to get a decent location.

The Two Towers: Asinelli and Garisenda

The Bologna Towers, also known as the Asinelli and Garisenda Towers, are two medieval towers in the Italian city of Bologna. They are Bologna's most recognized landmarks and a popular tourist attraction.

The Asinelli Tower, at 97.2 meters (319 feet), is the tallest of the two towers. The Asinelli family erected it between 1109 and 1119, and it was originally utilized as a watchtower and jail. The Garisenda Tower is 47 meters (154 feet) shorter. It was constructed at the same time as the Asinelli Tower, but it began to tilt soon after. The tower's tilting was finally halted by removing part of the base stones.

The Asinelli Tower is the only one of the two towers that is available to the public today.

The Two Towers are located in the center of Bologna, near the Piazza di Porta Ravegnana.

The Asinelli Tower has 498 steps to the top. The views from the top of the towers are stunning, providing panoramic views of Bologna.

Here are some tips for seeing the Two Towers:

- Purchase your tickets ahead of time, since the towers can become busy, especially during high season.
- Because there are many steps to climb, wear comfortable shoes.
- If you are terrified of heights, you should think twice about climbing the towers.
- Visit the towers for at least an hour.
- The Two Towers' hours of operation are as follows: 9:00 a.m. to 7:00 p.m. from April to September 9:00 a.m. to 6:00 p.m. from October to March
- On Mondays, the towers are closed.
- The admission fee to the Two Towers is: Adults pay €5, children (6-12 years) pay €3, and children under 6 years pay nothing.

While visiting the Two Towers, you can have the following life experiences:

- Climb to the top of the Asinelli Tower for 360-degree views of the city.
- Take a selfie with the Two Towers in the background
- Visit the museum in the Asinelli Tower, which displays medieval artifacts.

The Two Towers are a must-see for any Bologna visitor. They are a one-of-a-kind and iconic landmark that provides breathtaking views of the city. You can easily visit the towers and have a memorable experience with a little planning.

Here is my experience of visiting the Two Towers

I went to the Bologna Two Towers a few years ago. Their size and history impressed me. The Asinelli Tower is well worth climbing; the views from the top are spectacular. I would recommend visiting the towers early in the morning or late in the afternoon to avoid crowds. It can also get hot in the towers during the summer, so bring water and sunscreen.

Here are some other things to consider when visiting the Two Towers:

- The towers are in a busy part of town, so be prepared for crowds.
- Because there are no Elevators in the towers, you must climb the stairs.
- On a clear day, the views from the top of the towers are spectacular.
- The towers were constructed during a period of political and social upheaval in Bologna. They represented the power and wealth of the families who built them.
- The towers also served as defensive structures. They were armed and could be used to defend the city from an attack.
- The towers have appeared in numerous works of art and literature. They represent Bologna and its rich history.

Basilica di San Petronio

The Basilica di San Petronio in Bologna, Italy, is a large unfinished Catholic church. It is the largest church in Bologna and Italy's sixth-largest church. The building was started in 1390 to be the biggest church in the world, but development was suspended in the 17th century owing to a shortage of funding.

The Basilica di San Petronio is an outstanding example of Gothic architecture. The facade is three stories high and constructed of white marble. The lower level has pointed arches and columns. The middle level is embellished with saint and prophet figures. The upper level is incomplete.

The Basilica di San Petronio's interior is just as beautiful as its appearance. The nave is unusually long and wide, with pillars and arches lining it. The ceiling is constructed of wood and has paintings on it. The cathedral also contains several chapels, each of which is beautifully ornamented with artwork.

Traveling Suggestions

Here are a few tips for visitors to the Basilica di San Petronio:

- Purchase your tickets in advance, especially if you want to travel during peak season. Tickets can be purchased online or at the church's ticket office.

· Visit the church for at least an hour.

· Because there will be a lot of walking, wear comfortable shoes.

· If you want to understand more about the church's history, you may take a guided tour. English and Italian tours are provided.

· Be mindful of the church's religious essence. Dress correctly and speak quietly.

· Prices: Adults must pay €6 to enter the Basilica di San Petronio. Children, students, and the elderly can get discounted tickets.

· Time of Arrival and Closure: From Tuesday through Sunday, the Basilica di San Petronio is open from 8:30 a.m. to 1:30 p.m. and 3:00 p.m. to 6:30 p.m. On Mondays, the church is closed.

Archiginnasio of Bologna

The Archiginnasio di Bologna is a 16th-century building that was once the city's main university. It is located in the city center, on Piazza Galvani. The building was designed by Antonio Morandi, and construction began in 1562. It was completed in 1563 and consecrated the following year.

The Archiginnasio was originally designed to be a center of learning and culture. It housed schools, libraries, and lecture theaters. There was also a large anatomical theater where anatomy lessons were given. The anatomical theater is one of the most well-known features of the Archiginnasio. It is a circular theater with 300 seats. Murals portraying anatomical scenes decorate the walls of the theater.

The Archiginnasio ceased to be the principal university of Bologna in 1803. However, it was still used for educational purposes. In the early twentieth century, it was converted into a public library. The library is still housed in the Archiginnasio.

What is there to see and do?

The Archiginnasio is a fantastic site to see. There's a lot to see and do, including:

- The anatomical theater is the most noteworthy element of Archiginnasio. It is a circular theater with 300 seats. Murals portraying anatomical scenes decorate the walls of the theater.
- The Archiginnasio has a large public library. The library has about 800,000 books and manuscripts.
- The courtyard: The Archiginnasio's courtyard is gorgeous. The courtyard is surrounded by a loggia that is ornamented with coats of arms.
- The corridors: The Archiginnasio has numerous brilliantly painted passageways. The passages are decorated with frescoes and coats of arms.

Suggestions for Traveling

Here are some recommendations for Archiginnasio visitors:

- The Archiginnasio is open from 9 a.m. to 7 p.m. Tuesday through Sunday. Mondays are forbidden.
- The Archiginnasio entry fee for adults is €6.00. Students and minors pay a cheaper fee.
- In the anatomical theater, only guided tours are provided. The tours are available in both Italian and English.
- The library is available to the public for research purposes. However, you must make a reservation in advance.
- The Archiginnasio is a popular tourist destination.
- It is preferable to visit during the week because it is less congested.

Practical experience

When I visited the Archiginnasio a few years ago, I was pleased. The building is breathtaking, and the anatomical theater is a must-see. I recommend seeing the Archiginnasio if you're in Bologna.

Based on my own experience, here are some further suggestions:

- Spend at least 2 hours in the Archiginnasio.
- Because you will be walking a lot, choose comfortable shoes.
- Bring a camera to capture all of the exquisite elements of the structure.
- I recommend getting a guided tour if you want to understand more about Archiginnasio's history.

Neptune's Fountain

The Neptune Fountain was originally placed in Piazza Maggiore and was built in 1566. However, it was relocated.

The Neptune Fountain is huge in Bologna, Italy, located in Piazza del Nettuno, near Piazza Maggiore. It exemplifies the Mannerism of the Italian courtly class in the mid-sixteenth century.

Pope Pius IV commissioned the fountain in 1563, and it was created by the Flemish artist Giambologna. The Neptune statue is over four meters tall and weighs 2,200 kilos. It represents the Roman deity of the sea, Neptune, standing in a chariot carried by four sea horses. Other marine creatures, such as dolphins and tritons, adorn the fountain. It was moved to its current place in 1796.

What to see and do

The Neptune Fountain is one of Bologna's most recognizable monuments. It is a prominent tourist attraction and a must-see for every city visitor.

In addition to the Neptune monument, the fountain is adorned with various sculptures, such as:

- The four winds are represented by four sea horses.
- Dolphins symbolize the richness of the sea.
- Tritons are half-human, half-fish beings that serve as Neptune's servants.

The fountain is also flanked by a railing that features reliefs of sea animals.

Traveling Suggestions

Here are some tips for visitors to the Neptune Fountain:

- The Neptune Fountain is conveniently placed in the middle of Bologna.
- The fountain is open to the public for free.
- The fountain is best visited during the day when the sun shines and the fountain is lit.
- Because the fountain is a famous tourist attraction, it may get congested. To avoid crowds, go early in the morning or late in the evening.
- There are guided tours available if you want to understand more about the fountain's history.

Bologna's Porticoes

Bologna's porticoes are a network of covered walkways that stretch for nearly 66 kilometers (41 miles) across the city. They have nearly 4,000 arches and are the world's longest portico system. The porticoes were constructed over many centuries, beginning in the 11th century. They were built to provide shade from the heat and rain, but they have now become a symbol of the city.

Why are Bologna's porticoes so significant?

Bologna's porticoes are more than simply a method to keep dry in the weather. They play a crucial role in the history and culture of the city. They provide a feeling of community and connection and are popular gathering places for people to socialize, buy, and dine. The porticoes are also a popular tourist attraction, and they contribute to the distinctive character of Bologna.

Where are Bologna's porticoes?

Bologna's porticoes may be found throughout the city, although they are most concentrated in the old center. Some of the most well-known porticoes are:

- San Luca's Portico: This is the world's longest portico, reaching over 3,796 meters (2.35 miles). It goes from Porta Saragozza to the Madonna di San Luca Sanctuary atop the Colle della Guardia.
- San Petronio's Portico: This portico extends beside the Basilica of San Petronio, one of Italy's biggest churches.
- The Pavaglione Portico: This portico is situated in Piazza Maggiore, Bologna's largest plaza. It's a popular area for people-watching and eating al fresco.
- Portico dei Servi: This portico is situated on Strada Maggiore, one of Bologna's principal streets. It is surrounded by businesses and cafés.

How to Get to Bologna's Porticoes

Bologna's porticoes are conveniently accessible via public transit. The city center is serviced by a bus and tram network, with numerous stations positioned around the porticoes. You may also stroll or ride your bike to the porticoes.

Prices and hours of operation

Bologna's porticoes are open 24 hours a day, seven days a week. There are no admission costs.

Traveling Suggestions

Here are a few tips for visitors to Bologna's porticoes:

- Wear comfortable shoes since you will be walking a lot
- Bring a camera; you'll want to capture the porticoes' particular charm.
- Take your time and explore the porticos at your leisure.
- There are plenty of hidden jewels to be discovered
- Make a point of stopping to take in the scenery.
- Some of the nicest views of the city may be seen from the porticoes.
- If you're coming in the summer, the porticoes are an excellent way to cool down.
- Visit the porticoes at various times of the day to watch how they alter with the light.
- Discover the history of the porticoes and how they influenced the city.

Museums and Galleries

E xplore the fascinating world of Bologna's cultural tapestry by visiting its many museums and galleries. The National Gallery of Bologna is a testimony to Italy's rich cultural past, displaying treasures from throughout the ages. MAMbo, the Museum of Modern Art, on the other hand, takes a modern approach, displaying avant-garde pieces that defy traditions.

The Archaeological Museum is a treasure trove of ancient relics that unravel the city's past in detailed detail for those captivated by history's fascination. Meanwhile, the Museo Ducati celebrates the sleek and strong forms of Italian motorcycles, presenting an altogether other sort of artwork.

A visit to the Museum of the History of Bologna, which eloquently chronicles the city's development, would not be complete without a voyage through the city's creative tale. These institutions provide insights into many domains of creativity and history as travelers with a plethora of life experiences.

Intriguingly, these cultural hotspots jointly exemplify Bologna's vibrant art scene. Each museum, from classic to modern, archaeological to automotive, adds a unique thread to the rich cultural fabric of this lovely Italian city.

National Gallery of Bologna

The National Gallery of Bologna is a museum housed in the old Saint Ignatius Jesuit novitiate in the city's University Quarter, next to the Academy of Fine Arts. It holds around 1,300 paintings, sculptures, and other pieces of art spanning from the 13th to the 18th centuries.

- **Prices**: Admission is €8 for adults, €6 for children aged 6-18, students, and over 65s, and free for children under 6. Guided tours cost €10 for adults and €8 for students. €5 for an audio guide.
- **Amenities:** There is a café and a bookstore at the museum. You may leave your jackets and luggage in the cloakroom. The museum is handicapped accessible.
- **Location:** The Bologna National Gallery is situated at Via delle Belle Arti 56, Bologna. It is within a few minutes' walk from Piazza Maggiore and the Two Towers.
- **Hours of operation:** Tuesday and Wednesday: 9:00 a.m. to 2:00 p.m. (last admission at 1:00 p.m.) Thursday through Sunday and holidays: 9:00 a.m. to 7:00 p.m. (last entry at 6:00 p.m.)

Personal experience

On a recent trip to Italy, I visited the Bologna National Gallery. The vastness and elegance of the museum initially wowed me. The collection is well-curated, and the artworks are exhibited in an easy-to-appreciate manner.

I spent around two hours in the museum and could easily have spent longer. I was especially drawn to the works of Bolognese painters such as Giotto, Raphael, and Guido Reni. I also liked the sculptures and other pieces of art in the collection.

I had a fantastic day visiting the National Gallery of Bologna. Anyone interested in art history or Italian culture should go.

MAMbo - Museum of Modern Art

The MAMbo - Museo d'Arte Moderna di Bologna is a modern and contemporary art museum in Bologna, Italy. It opened in 2007 and is located in a former bakery. The museum's collection comprises about 5,000 pieces of art dating from the conclusion of WWII to the current day. Paintings, sculptures, sketches, photos, and films are among the works in the collection.

Permanent Collection

The MAMbo's permanent collection is composed of three major sections:

The Italian Section: Works by Italian artists from the 1950s to the present are included in this section. This section features artists such as Lucio Fontana, Piero Manzoni, and Mario Merz.

The International Area: From the 1960s to the present, this area features works by artists from all over the globe. Andy Warhol, Jeff Koons, and Damien Hirst are among the artists covered in this area.

The Experimental area: Works in this area are believed to be on the cutting edge of contemporary art. Marina Abramović, Takashi Murakami, and Ai Weiwei are among the artists covered in this area.

Temporary Exhibitions

The MAMbo, in addition to its permanent collection, presents temporary exhibits of contemporary art. These shows, which rotate every few months, showcase the work of both renowned and young artists.

Amenities

Visitors to the MAMbo may enjoy a variety of facilities, including:

- A library with a variety of books and publications on modern and con-temporary art A shop selling books, posters, and other museum-related items
- A café and restaurant that serves food and beverages.
- A gift store selling museum-related souvenirs and gifts.

Hours and Location

The MAMbo is situated in Via Don Minzoni 14, in the heart of Bologna. It is open from 10:00 a.m. to 6:30 p.m., Tuesday through Sunday. Visitors are not permitted on Mondays and public holidays.

Entry Fee:

The MAMbo entry fee is €6 for adults, €4 for discounted tickets, and free for children under the age of 12. Tickets are available for purchase either online or at the museum's ticket office.

Useful Information

The MAMbo is a vast museum, so plan on spending at least two hours there. The museum is wheelchair accessible, and audio tours in English, Italian, French, German, and Spanish are available.

Personal Experience

I visited the MAMbo a few years ago and was blown away by the collection. The Italian Section, which contains some of my favorite pieces of art, such as Lucio Fontana's "Concetto Spaziale, Attese" and Piero Manzoni's "Achrome," was extremely appealing to me. The temporary exhibition I visited was also quite intriguing to me. It was about the work of Japanese artist Yayoi Kusama, and it was quite interesting.

Archaeological Museum

The Museo Civico Archeologico di Bologna (Archaeological Civic Museum of Bologna) is one of the most important archaeological museums in Italy. It is located in the heart of the city, in the 15th-century Palazzo Galvani. The museum's collection spans from prehistory to the Roman era and includes a wide variety of artifacts from the local area, as well as from other parts of Italy and the Mediterranean world.

Collections

The museum's collections are divided into four major categories:

- **Prehistory and protohistory:** This section includes artifacts from the Stone Age, Bronze Age, and Iron Age, including tools, weapons, jewelry, and pottery.
- **Etruscan collection:** This section is one of the museum's most important, and includes a wide variety of artifacts from the Etruscan civilization, which flourished in the Po Valley from the 8th to the 1st centuries BC. Highlights include the Chimera of Bologna, a bronze statuette of a mythical creature with the head of a lion, the body of a goat, and the tail of a snake; and the Sarcophagus of the Spouses, a painted terracotta sarcophagus from the 4th century BC.
- **Roman collection:** This section includes artifacts from the Roman period, including sculptures, mosaics, and pottery. Highlights include the Head of Medusa, a marble sculpture from the 1st century AD, and the Ara Pacis, a large marble altar dedicated to peace, which was originally located in the Forum of Augustus in Rome.
- **Egyptian collection:** This section includes a small but important collection of Egyptian antiquities, including mummies, sarcophagi, and jewelry.

Other amenities

The museum also has a number of other amenities, including a library, a bookstore, and a cafe. There is also a temporary exhibition space, which hosts rotating exhibitions of archaeological artifacts from around the world.

Location and opening hours

The museum is located at Via dell'Archiginnasio 2, in the heart of Bologna. It is open from 9:00 to 18:00 on Tuesdays to Sundays.

Entry Fee

Admission is €10 for adults, €8 for seniors and students, and free for children under 18.

Museo Ducati

The Museo Ducati is a museum devoted to the Ducati motorcycle company's history. It is situated in Borgo Panigale, Bologna, Italy, near the Ducati facility. The museum, which opened in 1998, has a collection of over 200 bikes as well as various exhibits relating to Ducati's history.

Prices and Extras

The Museo Ducati admission charge is €13 for adults, €11 for pensioners and students, and €9 for children under the age of 14. A family ticket for two adults and two children costs €36. From Tuesday through Sunday, the museum is open from 10:00 to 18:00. Mondays and holidays are not permitted.

There is a gift store in the museum where you may purchase Ducati products such as apparel, souvenirs, and motorbike components. On the grounds, there is also a coffee and a restaurant.

Location

Via Antonio Cavalieri Ducati 3, 40132 Bologna, Italy is the address of the Museo Ducati. The Bologna Centrale railway station is roughly a 15-minute walk away. You may also catch the museum bus number 13 from the railway station.

Hours of Operation and Closure

From Tuesday to Sunday, the Museo Ducati is open from 10:00 to 18:00. Mondays and holidays are not permitted.

Exhibits

The Ducati Museum is organized into four major sections:

- **Ducati Moments:** A collection of exhibitions, including bikes, racing vehicles, and pictures, explain the narrative of Ducati.
- **The Road Bikes:** This section showcases Ducati's previous and contemporary road bikes.
- **The Racing Bikes:** This section features Ducati's racing bikes, including World Championship-winning models.
- **The Innovation Gallery:** This section delves into the technical breakthroughs that have propelled Ducati to the forefront of the motorcycle industry.

Other Interests

Aside from the displays, the Museo Ducati provides several different activities, such as:

- Visitors may enjoy a guided tour of the Ducati plant to learn how the bikes are created.
- Riding Experience: Visitors may try out a Ducati motorbike.
- Simulator Experience: Visitors may simulate racing a Ducati motorbike on a simulator.

Museum of the History of Bologna

The Museum of Bologna History (Museo della Storia di Bologna) is an Italian museum devoted to the history of the city of Bologna. It is housed in the Palazzo Pepoli Vecchio, a historic palace in Bologna's downtown. The museum, which opened in 2012, has about 10,000 objects, including archaeological findings, artworks, and documents.

Prices and Amenities:

The Museum of Bologna's History costs €10 for adults, €8 for pensioners and students, and €6 for children under 14. A family ticket for two adults and two children costs €28. From Tuesday through Sunday, the museum is open from 10:00 to 18:00. Mondays and holidays are not permitted.

The museum offers a gift store where you may purchase souvenirs and publications about Bologna's history. On the site, there is also a café.

Location

The Museum of Bologna's History is situated at Via Castiglione 8, 40124 Bologna, Italy. The Bologna Centrale railway station is roughly a 10-minute walk away. You may also catch the museum bus number 30 from the railway station.

Hours of Operation and Closure

The Museum of Bologna History is open from 10:00 a.m. to 6:00 p.m., Tuesday through Sunday. Mondays and holidays are not permitted.

Exhibits

The Museum of Bologna History is composed of three sections:

1. **The History of Bologna**: This part describes the city's history from its beginnings until the Middle Ages.
2. **Bologna throughout the Renaissance and Baroque periods**: This part delves into the city's golden era when it was a prominent center of art, learning, and culture.
3. **Modern and Contemporary Bologna:** This part covers the history of the city from the nineteenth century to the present.

The museum's exhibits are highly interactive, using a range of media such as movies, interactive displays, and hands-on activities to convey the narrative of Bologna. Throughout the year, there are also several special exhibits.

Exploring Bologna's Art Scene

Street Art

Wandering the streets and looking for street art is one of the best ways to discover Bologna's art culture. Murals and graffiti may be seen across the city, from the historic core to the more industrial regions.

Here are some of the greatest sites in Bologna to discover street art:

- **Quadrilatero:** A variety of stunning paintings can be seen in this medieval market sector.
- **Via del Pratello:** This street is well-known for its counterculture movement and is home to a lot of murals painted by local artists.
- **Porta Galliera:** One of the city's oldest gates, it is adorned with a multitude of paintings.
- **Via Zamboni:** The University of Bologna is located on this street, which has several paintings created by student painters.
- **Sant'Eufemia:** This church is embellished with paintings by Bolognese artist Francesco Francia.

Contemporary Art Galleries

A variety of modern art galleries can also be found in Bologna. Here are some of our favorites:

MAMbo - Museo d'Arte Moderna di Bologna: This modern and contemporary art museum is housed in a former Bologna slaughterhouse. Over 4,000 pieces of art, including paintings, sculptures, and installations, are housed at the museum.

CAI - Centro Arti Visive Internazionali: This contemporary art center organizes international art exhibits regularly. The institution is housed in the historic Santa Maria della Vita church.

The Galleria Il Bisonte: This focuses on modern Italian art.

Galleria Continua: This gallery has many sites worldwide, including one in Bologna. The gallery exhibits both renowned and new artists' work.

Spazio Gerra: This gallery promotes the work of young and rising artists.

Helpful Tips:

- When the weather is nice, the ideal time to visit Bologna for street art is in the spring or autumn.
- Wear comfy shoes because you will be walking a lot.
- Bring a camera to record all of the incredible art you see.
- Inquire with locals about their best sites for street art.
- To discover the greatest murals, use the Bologna Street Art Map.

Culinary Delights

B egin a delectable trip through the gastronomic tapestry of Bologna, a city famed for its Bolognese food that tantalizes the taste buds and embodies the spirit of Italian gastronomy. Within the domain of "Bolognese Cuisine: A Culinary Journey," discriminating palates will find a world of tastes and traditions.

Venture into the heart of this culinary paradise to experience the rich melody of Traditional Dishes and Local Specialties. From the classic tagliatelle al ragù to the savory mortadella, each dish offers a narrative of time-honored traditions and painstaking workmanship. But where can you locate these delicacies? Discover the answer as you explore the city's hidden culinary jewels and uncover Where to Eat the Best Pasta in Bologna.

A truly epicurean excursion would not be complete without visiting the Mercato di Mezzo, a bustling marketplace brimming with the finest vegetables and fragrant spices. The busy food booths and conversations of local sellers bring the essence of Bologna to life.

Wine and Food Tours visit the gorgeous vineyards and cellars, presenting a wonderful mix of regional wines and exquisite snacks. Cooking Classes and Food Experiences provide the chance to learn the skill of preparing traditional Bolognese cuisine, creating memories to relish long after the tour ends.

Whether you're a seasoned traveler or looking for new experiences, Bologna's gastronomic pleasures guarantee an unparalleled blend of cuisine, culture, and history that will definitely leave an everlasting impact on your senses.

Bolognese Cuisine: A Culinary Journey

A culinary tour to Bologna should begin with a visit to the city's oldest and biggest market, the Mercato di Mezzo. Fresh fruit, meats, cheeses, and other components for the ideal Bolognese sauce may be found here. Try some of the regional delicacies, such as mortadella (cured pig sausage), culatello (dry-cured ham), and tortellini (stuffed pasta).

When you've gathered all of your ingredients, it's time to cook the Bolognese sauce. Ground beef, pork, pancetta, carrots, celery, onions, tomatoes, and white wine are all used in the classic recipe. For many hours, the sauce is slowly simmered until it is thick and aromatic.

Tagliatelle, a flat pasta similar to fettuccine, is commonly served with Bolognese sauce. Tortellini in brodo (tortellini in broth), lasagne (a layered pasta dish with meat sauce, béchamel sauce, and cheese), and cappellacci di zucca (pumpkin-filled pasta) are other typical Bologna pasta dishes.

Without dessert, no supper in Bologna would be complete. Zuppa Inglese (a trifle-like dessert prepared with sponge cake, custard, and amaretto), crème fritta (fried custard), and tortellini di riso (rice-filled pastry) are among the city's most renowned sweets.

Here are some tips for eating Bolognese like a local:

- Visit a traditional trattoria. These eateries provide home-cooked meals at reasonable prices.
- Get the house special. This is often the greatest way to sample the local food.
- Request suggestions from your waiter. They would gladly assist you in

selecting the ideal food.

- Don't be frightened to attempt new things. Bologna is a culinary innovator's city, therefore there are many fresh and intriguing foods to taste.

Here are several restaurants in Bologna that serve true Bolognese cuisine:

Osteria del Sole: Since 1465, this restaurant has served authentic Bolognese cuisine.

Trattoria Il Sorriso: Known for its home-cooked pasta dishes, Trattoria Il Sorriso is a family-run establishment.

Il Latini: This is a more premium restaurant, but the cuisine is still great.

La Griglia di Varrone: This grilled meat and vegetable restaurant is located in Varrone.

Quadrilatero d'Oro: This market district is filled with modest businesses and restaurants providing typical Bolognese cuisine.

A gastronomic trip to Bologna is a sensory overload. This city offers everything for everyone, from the freshest ingredients to the most delectable cuisine.

Here are some more details on food costs in Bologna:

- A conventional trattoria supper will normally cost between €15 and €20 per person.
- A pasta plate in a restaurant will cost between €8 and €10.
- A glass of wine will cost between €2 and €3.
- Dessert will cost around €5-6.
- Prices will, of course, vary based on the establishment and the food. However, food in Bologna is rather inexpensive. As a result, you may have a delectable supper without breaking the wallet.

Traditional Dishes and Local Specialties

Here are some of Bologna's classic foods and regional delicacies:

Tagliatelle al ragù: This is Bologna's most renowned dish, created with hand-rolled pasta and a slow-cooked beef sauce. The sauce is generally prepared with beef, hog, and veal, although vegetarian variants are now available.

Brodo Tortellini: This is another traditional Bologna dish that consists of miniature, filled pasta dumplings in a broth. The classic filling consists of pork, mortadella, and Parmigiano Reggiano cheese, however, there are additional options.

Lasagna Bolognese: This pasta dish is stacked with ragù sauce, bechamel sauce, and Parmigiano Reggiano cheese. It is comparable to the more well-known lasagna bolognese, although the Bolognese version has thinner spaghetti and a less rich sauce.

Mortadella: Mortadella is a cured pig sausage prepared with finely ground meat, spices, and pistachios. It's a common ingredient in many Bologna dishes, including the mortadella sandwich.

Parmigiano Reggiano (Parmigiano Reggiano): This is a sort of dry, hard cheese manufactured from cow's milk. It is one of the most well-known cheeses in Italy and is used in a variety of savory and sweet dishes.

Tigelle: These are little, spherical flatbreads made on a griddle. They are often accompanied with a variety of fillings, such as cured meats, cheeses, or vegetables.

Fritte crescione: These are little fried breads prepared from a variety of flour known as crescione. They are often accompanied with a dipping sauce, such as ragu or pesto.

Spritz: This is an alcoholic drink created with prosecco, Aperol, and soda water. It is a popular drink in Bologna, and it is often served as an aperitif.

Lambrusco: This is a red wine produced from the Lambrusco vine. It's a light, fruity wine that's best served chilled.

Where to Enjoy the Best Pasta in Bologna

Trattoria del Tempo Buono: This dining establishment is well-known for its typical Bolognese fare, which includes handmade pasta. Prices vary from €10 and €20 per person.

Sfoglina Rosella: This restaurant is a local favorite because of its delicious pasta and courteous service. Prices per person vary from €12 to €25.

Osteria Bottega Portici: This restaurant is housed in a lovely old arcade and serves a wide range of pasta dishes as well as other typical Emilia-Romagna fare. Prices per person vary from €15 to €30.

Trattoria Il Pagliaccio: This restaurant is well-known for its creative twists on classic pasta meals. Prices per person vary from €18 to €35.

Da Cesare al Casaletto: This restaurant is a little more pricey, but it is well worth it given the high quality of the cuisine. The pasta is prepared fresh every day, and the sauces are entirely homemade. Prices per person vary from €25 to €40.

Exploring the Mercato di Mezzo

The Mercato di Mezzo is a covered market in Bologna's historic center. It is one of the city's oldest and biggest marketplaces, having been in operation since the Middle Ages. Fresh fruit, meats, cheeses, and other food products may be found at the market. It's also a popular shopping spot for residents.

The food market and the non-food market are separated at the Mercato di Mezzo. The food market is on the ground level and has a large range of vendors offering fresh fruit, meats, cheeses, and other culinary products. The non-food market sits on the top level and offers a wide range of products, including apparel, souvenirs, and home items.

The Mercato di Mezzo is an excellent location to learn about local culture and food. It's also a wonderful spot to get amazing deals on food and other items. If you want to have a one-of-a-kind and genuine shopping experience in Bologna, the Mercato di Mezzo is a terrific place to start.

Here are some tips for navigating the Mercato di Mezzo:

- Begin your tour of the food market. This is where you'll discover the freshest fruits, vegetables, meats, and cheeses.
- Do not be frightened to bargain. This is a regular technique in Italian marketplaces, and you may be able to negotiate a lower price.
- Take your time and absorb the surroundings. The Mercato di Mezzo is a busy market where you can people-watch.
- Try some of the local cuisine. There are several food kiosks offering items you may not have tasted before. Try some of the regional favorites, such as mortadella or tortellini.
- Bring some cash. The Mercato di Mezzo does not take credit cards at several of its booths.
- Keep an eye on your surroundings. The Mercato di Mezzo is a crowded site, so be careful of your surroundings and keep your possessions close to hand.

Here are some more things to consider before visiting the Mercato di Mezzo:

- The market is open from 7:00 a.m. to 1:30 p.m., Monday through Saturday.
- Early in the morning is the ideal time to come since the market is at its freshest.

- The market is in the pedestrian-only Quadrilatero district of Bologna.
- Near the market, there are a lot of restaurants and cafés where you can eat after your shopping.

Wine and Food Tours

The city is home to several world-class restaurants and produces some of the country's best wines.

In Bologna, there are numerous wine and food tours to suit all budgets and interests.

Here are a few of the most common options:

- The Taste Bologna Food Tour is a 3-hour walking tour that takes you to some of the best restaurants in the city. Traditional Bolognese dishes such as tortellini in brodo, mortadella, and gelato will be served. The tour also includes a stop at a local wine bar to learn about the region's wines and sample a few different varieties. This excursion costs €45 per person.
- The 4-hour Italian Days Food Experience includes visits to a local winery and a traditional restaurant. You'll learn about the winemaking process and sample some local wines. A four-course meal with wine pairings will be served at the restaurant. This excursion costs €180 per person.
- The Delicious Bologna Food Tour is a three-hour walking tour of the city's hidden gems. You'll get to try dishes like tigelle, crescentine, and ragù alla bolognese that you might not find elsewhere. The tour also includes a stop at a local market to learn about the fresh produce used in Bologna's cuisine. This tour costs €35.00 per person.

These are just a few of the numerous wine and food tours offered in Bologna. When selecting a tour, keep your budget, interests, and time constraints in mind.

Here is some additional useful information to consider when planning a wine and food tour in Bologna:

- The majority of tours are conducted in the morning or afternoon.
- It is advisable to book your tour ahead of time, especially during peak season.
- Put on comfortable shoes because you will be walking a lot.
- Bring a camera to document your experiences.
- Prepare to try a lot of food and wine!

Cooking Classes and Food Experiences

In Bologna, there are a range of culinary lessons and gourmet experiences to suit all budgets and interests. Here are a few of the most common options:

Cesarine: We're a small bunch. Bologna Pasta and Tiramisu Class: This workshop teaches how to cook typical Bolognese pasta dishes including tagliatelle al ragù and tortellini in brodo. The workshop will take place at the house of a local Bolognese cook, who will teach you the secrets of her family's recipes. The cost of the course is €65 per participant.

Bologna Cooking Class: This session provides a more in-depth introduction to Bolognese cuisine. You'll learn how to create anything from pasta to risotto to grilled meats. The program is given by a skilled chef in a professional kitchen. The cost of the course is €85 per participant.

Tasty Bologna Cooking Class and Food Tour with Chef Antonino: This is an excellent choice for anyone interested in learning about Bologna's cuisine and culture. The program starts with a trip to the Mercato delle Erbe, a typical market where you will learn about the fresh ingredients utilized in Bologna cuisine. Then you'll head to Chef Antonino's house to learn how to create a typical Bolognese meal. The lesson concludes with a meal prepared by you. The cost of the course is €125 per participant.

These are just a handful of the many cooking workshops and culinary experiences offered in Bologna. When selecting a class, keep your budget, interests, and time limits in mind.

Here is some more useful information to consider while organizing a cooking lesson or cuisine experience in Bologna:

- The majority of sessions are held in the morning or afternoon.
- It is best to reserve your lesson ahead of time, particularly during the high season.
- Wear comfy clothing since you will be cooking.
- Bring a camera to document your experiences.
- Prepare to have a great time!

Here are some more suggestions for selecting a cooking lesson or cuisine experience in Bologna:

- Read internet reviews to obtain a sense of the class's or experience's quality.
- Request suggestions from the personnel at your hotel or hostel.
- Consider the class's or experience's location. Choose a lesson or event that is conveniently located if you are short on time.
- If you are traveling in a group, be sure to schedule a lesson or event that can fit the number of people in your party.

Day Trips and Nearby Attractions

S et out on an enthralling discovery of Bologna's surrounding gems with a variety of interesting day excursions and adjacent sites. Explore the heart of Modena, known as the Land of Balsamic Vinegar, and discover the age-old artistry of this beautiful elixir. Parma, a real Gourmet's Paradise, offers indulgence with gastronomic delicacies that will satisfy even the most discriminating palates.

In Ravenna, a historic city, beautiful mosaics and Byzantine artifacts beckon, providing a glimpse into a bygone period. Meanwhile, Ferrara's Renaissance glory, showing architectural wonders and eternal beauty, is a tribute to its rich cultural legacy.

The Apennines provide amazing outdoor adventures for the passionate explorer, from wandering lush woods to immersing oneself in nature's embrace. For wine aficionados, the Emilia-Romagna region's vineyard excursions provide an opportunity to sample the best wines while taking in the lovely scenery.

Modena: The Land of Balsamic Vinegar

Modena is an Italian city in the Emilia-Romagna region known for its balsamic vinegar and motor racing. The city is about 100 kilometers south of Bologna.

Traditional Modena balsamic vinegar (Aceto Balsamico Tradizionale di Modena) is a condiment created from grape must (the sweet juice of freshly squeezed grapes) that has been kept for at least 12 years in a succession of oak barrels. The maturing process imparts the vinegar's distinctive sweet, tangy, and nuanced taste.

Here are some hands-on activities in Modena to learn more about balsamic vinegar:

- Visit a balsamic vinegar production or acetaia. This is the most often used method for learning about balsamic vinegar. In Modena, there are several acetaie that give tours and tastings. This is an excellent opportunity to learn about the manufacturing process and sample many kinds of vinegar.
- Attend a culinary lesson. Many culinary workshops in Modena use balsamic vinegar in their menus. This is an excellent method for learning how to utilize balsamic vinegar in your cuisine.
- Visit the Modena Balsamico Tradizionale Museum. This museum chronicles the history of balsamic vinegar from its beginnings to the present. At the museum, you can also observe and taste many types of balsamic vinegar.
- Attend the Balsamic Vinegar Festival every year. Every year in October, Modena hosts this event. Balsamic vinegar is celebrated through tastings, seminars, and other activities,

Parma: A Gourmet's Paradise

Parma is a city in Italy's Emilia-Romagna region known for its food and culture. The city is approximately 100 kilometers south of Bologna.

Parma is well-known for:

Prosciutto di Parma: This world-renowned ham is made from the hind legs of specially bred pigs raised in Emilia-Romagna. The ham has been dry-cured for at least a year and has a delicate, sweet flavor.

Parmigiano-Reggiano: Made from cow's milk, this hard cheese has a nutty, sharp flavor. It has been aged for at least 12 months and is frequently used in grating.

Balsamic vinegar: This sweet and sour vinegar is made from grape must that has been aged for at least 12 years in a series of wooden barrels. It is frequently used as a condiment and in cooking.

Culatello: This cured ham is made from a boned pig thigh that has been stuffed into a casing. It has a rich, fatty flavor and has been aged for at least 6 months.

Tortelli di zucca: Pumpkin and ricotta cheese fill these pasta dumplings. They are frequently accompanied by a sage butter sauce.

Here are some hands-on activities you can do in Parma to learn more about its cuisine:

- Visit a cheese or prosciutto producer. In Parma, many prosciutto and cheese producers offer tours and tastings. This is an excellent opportunity to learn about the manufacturing process and sample various product varieties.
- Attend a cooking class. In Parma, numerous cooking classes use local ingredients. This is an excellent way to learn to cook like a local.
- Go to FICO Eataly World. This is a food-themed park with restaurants, shops, and exhibits devoted to Italian cuisine. It is an excellent place to learn about Italian cuisine and sample various regional dishes.
- Participate in the annual Food & Wine Festival. Every year in September, Parma hosts this festival. There are tastings, workshops, and other events celebrating Emilia-Romagna food and wine.

Ravenna: Mosaics and Byzantine Treasures

Ravenna is a UNESCO World Heritage Site known for its beautiful mosaics found in many of the city's churches and buildings. The city was once the capital of the Western Roman Empire and, later, the Byzantine Empire in Italy. The architecture and art of the city reflect the city's rich history.

Some of Ravenna's most famous mosaics can be found in the following locations:

Mausoleum of Galla Placidia: This 5th-century mausoleum contains some of the best-preserved early Christian mosaics. Intricate mosaics depicting religious scenes cover the walls and ceiling.

Basilica of San Vitale: This Byzantine mosaic masterpiece dates from the sixth century. Mosaics depicting biblical scenes and figures adorn the walls and ceiling.

Sant'Apollinare Nuovo Basilica: This 6th-century church is famous for its mosaics depicting Jesus Christ's life.

Basilica of Sant'Apollinare Nuovo: This 6th-century church, located just outside the city center, is famous for its mosaics depicting the Virgin Mary and saints.

Ravenna, in addition to its mosaics, has several other attractions, including:

The Archiepiscopal Palace: This 8th-century palace houses several important artifacts, including the Orthodox Baptistery and the Neonian Mausoleum.

The National Museum of Ravenna: This museum houses an archaeological collection from the city, including mosaics, sculptures, and pottery.

The Roman Theater: Built in the first century AD, this theater is one of the best-preserved Roman theaters in Italy.

Ravenna is a small city, but it is jam-packed with sights and activities. Ravenna is a must-see for anyone interested in Byzantine art and architecture.

Here are some activities you can do in Ravenna:

- Take a tour of the city's mosaics with a guide. This is an excellent way to learn about the mosaics' history and significance.
- Visit the Ravenna National Museum. This museum houses an archaeological collection from the city, including mosaics, sculptures, and pottery.
- Attend an opera or a concert at the Teatro Alighieri. This theater, which is located in the city center, hosts a variety of performances throughout the year.
- Take a boat ride through the Canal Candiano. This canal provides spectacular views of the city and its surroundings.

Here are some tips for getting practical experience in Ravenna:

- Plan ahead of time for tours and tickets, especially during peak season.
- Put on comfortable shoes, considering that you will be walking a lot.
- Bring a camera to document your experiences.
- Entrance fees can be costly, so be prepared to spend some money.

Ferrara: A Renaissance Gem

Ferrara, a UNESCO World Heritage Site, is well-known for its stunning Renaissance architecture. From the 13th through the 18th century, the Este dynasty dominated the city, and it became a prominent center of art and culture during this period.

Some of Ferrara's most prominent Renaissance structures may be located

in the following locations:

The Este Castle: was erected in the 14th century and is one of Italy's biggest and most spectacular fortresses.

The Ducal Palace: Built in the 15th century, this palace houses several notable pieces of art, including paintings by Titian and Raphael.

The Schifanoia Palace: was erected in the 15th century and has murals by Cosmé Tura and Francesco del Cossa.

The Cathedral of Ferrara: Built in the 12th century, this cathedral is noted for its Romanesque and Gothic architecture.

Ferrara, in addition to its Renaissance architecture, features a variety of additional attractions, including:

The Jewish Ghetto: Established in the 16th century, this ghetto is one of Europe's oldest and best-preserved Jewish ghettos.

The Natural History Museum: This museum holds a collection of over one million plant, animal, and mineral specimens.

The Botanical Garden: Founded in the 17th century, this garden has flora from all over the globe.

Ferrara is a tiny city, yet there is enough to see and do. Ferrara is a must-see for anybody interested in Renaissance art and architecture.

Here are some activities you can do in Ferrara:

- Take a tour of the city's Renaissance architecture with a guide. This is an excellent approach to learning about the structures' history and importance.

- Explore Este Castle and Ducal Palace. These palaces house some of the city's most notable pieces of art.
- Attend an opera or a concert at the Teatro Comunale. This theater, which is situated in the city center, features a variety of acts throughout the year.
- Take a tour through the Jewish Ghetto. This is a fantastic location to learn about the history of Ferrara's Jewish community.
- The Botanical Garden and the Natural History Museum are well worth a visit. These museums are excellent places to learn about nature.

Here are some tips for getting hands-on experience in Ferrara:

- Plan ahead of time for tours and tickets, particularly during peak season.
- Put on comfortable shoes, since you will be walking a lot.
- Bring a camera to document your experiences.
- Entrance fees might be costly, so be prepared to pay some money.

Outdoor Adventures in the Apennines

The Apennines are an excellent location for outdoor activities. The mountains provide breathtaking views, demanding treks, and several possibilities for leisure.

Some of the most popular outdoor activities in the Apennines include:

Hiking: The Apennines include a wide range of hiking paths, from short strolls to strenuous climbs. The Sentiero Italia, the Alta Via dei Parchi, and the Via degli Dei are among the most popular hiking paths.

Mountain biking: The Apennines have various mountain bike tracks ranging from beginner to expert level. The Sentiero della Bonifica, the Sentiero delle Gravine, and the Sentiero dei Briganti are among the most popular mountain bike paths.

Rock climbing: The Apennines are also a renowned rock climbing location. There are several climbing places with routes for climbers of various skill levels. The Monti Sibillini, Majella National Park, and the Gran Sasso National Park are among the most popular climbing sites.

Winter sports: Winter sports such as skiing and snowboarding are popular in the Apennines. There are several ski resorts in the mountains, offering slopes for all skill levels. The Terminillo, Roccaraso, and Campo Imperatore are among the most popular ski resorts.

Here are some tips for enjoying a safe and pleasurable trip to the Apennines:

- Plan your vacation ahead of time: This is particularly crucial if you want to go trekking or climbing since you will need to reserve accommodations and permits ahead of time.
- Keep an eye on the weather conditions: The weather in the Apennines may change fast, so be prepared for any situation.
- Dress for the occasion: Dress in layers so you can adapt to changing temperatures.
- Bring lots of water and food with you: It is critical to keep hydrated and energetic when trekking or climbing.
- Inform someone of your plans: This is particularly crucial if you want to hike or climb in distant locations.
- Keep an eye on your surroundings: Keep an eye out for animals and other potential threats.
- Remove all traces: Respect the environment by packing out what you bring in.

Vineyard Tours in the Emilia-Romagna Region

Emilia-Romagna is famous for its great cuisine and wine. The area is home to some of Italy's most renowned vineyards, including Barolo, Barbaresco, and Lambrusco.

Some of the most popular vineyard excursions in Emilia-Romagna include:

Barolo and Barbaresco Wine Tour: This journey brings you to the heart of the wine districts of Barolo and Barbaresco. You will tour various vineyards and learn about how these world-renowned wines are made.

Lambrusco Wine Tour: This excursion takes you to the wine area of Lambrusco. You'll go to many vineyards and learn about the process of making this famous sparkling wine.

Emilia-Romagna Food and Wine Tour: This trip includes stops at vineyards and food producers. You will learn about the regional cuisine and taste some of its most renowned dishes.

Motorcycle and Wine Tour: This trip combines a motorbike ride through the countryside of Emilia-Romagna with visits to numerous wineries.

Tasting Menu and Wine Pairing: A tasting meal at a Michelin-starred restaurant matched with wines from the area is included in this package.

Here are some tips for getting hands-on experience on a vineyard tour in Emilia-Romagna:

- Plan ahead of time for your tour: This is particularly crucial during peak season.
- Wear comfortable shoes since you will be walking a lot.
- Bring a camera: You'll want to record your tour recollections.
- Be willing to try new things: The Emilia-Romagna area produces a wide range of wines, so sample a few.
- Inquire: The winemakers would gladly answer any questions you may have concerning the winemaking process.

Shopping and Souvenir

E xploring the dynamic city of Bologna provides visitors with an enthralling shopping experience that expertly balances history and innovation. The shopping districts of Bologna are a treasure trove for anyone looking for a true flavor of Italian culture. Stepping into these areas is like taking a trip back in time, where busy marketplaces and lovely artisan stores show the soul of the city.

Local markets and artisan shops reveal a world of handmade pleasures, ranging from scrumptious gastronomic treats to magnificent leather products. The rich culinary legacy of the city comes to life in its markets, where fresh vegetables, fragrant spices, and aged cheeses entice discriminating palates. Aside from cuisine, craftsmen display their talents in jewelry, pottery, and textiles, providing one-of-a-kind keepsakes of Bologna's enchantment.

Fashion and design boutiques cater to consumers with a keen sense of style, reflecting Italy's legendary fashion skills. Boutique windows here showcase a blend of classic workmanship and modern design, with everything from fitted suits to avant-garde accessories available. The retail environment in Bologna exemplifies Italy's impact on worldwide fashion.

No vacation to Bologna is complete without purchasing Souvenirs to Take Home that capture the character of the city. From locally made wines to delicate pottery, these mementos capture the character of the city. The fascination is found not only in the goods themselves but also in the tales they contain—each piece is a tangible recollection of a stroll through Bologna's intriguing streets. Bologna's shops and souvenirs give an enlightening insight into the city's character for guests seeking an immersed experience, assuring treasured memories for years to come.

Bologna's Shopping Districts

The city is also a popular shopping destination, with shops to suit all budgets and tastes.

Here are some of Bologna's most popular retail districts:

Via Indipendenza: This is Bologna's major shopping street. It has a mix of high-end and mid-range retailers, as well as cheap alternatives.

Galleria Cavour: This is a covered shopping arcade featuring a variety of retailers, including fashion, jewelry, and homewares.

Quadrilatero: This is a historic neighborhood with tiny lanes dotted with boutiques, antique stores, and cafés.

Porta Nuova (New Port): This is a more trendy neighborhood with a mix of independent shops and designer businesses.

Mezzanine Market: This is a typical market with fresh fruit, meats, cheeses, and other regional specialties.

Here are some tips for getting hands-on experience in Bologna's retail districts:

Expect to haggle: This is particularly frequent in the Quadrilatero neighborhood.

Don't be hesitant to ask for a discount: Many retailers will negotiate pricing, particularly if you purchase many things.

Keep an eye on your surroundings: Pickpocketing is a problem in several places in Bologna, so keep your possessions close at hand.

Have fun with it: Shopping in Bologna is an excellent opportunity to learn about the city's culture and history.

Here are some more helpful hints for arranging a shopping trip to Bologna:

- The ideal time to shop in Bologna is during the week, when the streets are less busy.
- There are several shopping trips available, so choose one that matches your interests and budget.
- If you are on a tight budget, the Quadrilatero area has numerous hidden beauties.
- If you want a more luxurious shopping experience, head to the Via Indipendenza district.

Local Markets and Artisan Shops

There are also a variety of local markets and artisan stores in the city where you may purchase unique gifts, fresh fruit, and delectable cuisine.

Here are some of Bologna's most popular local markets and artisan shops:

The Mercato delle Erbe: This is a covered market in the center of Bologna. It is an excellent source of fresh fruit, meats, cheeses, and other regional delights.

Mercato di Mezzo: This is an open-air market in the Quadrilatero neighborhood. It is an excellent location for purchasing souvenirs, apparel, and other local things.

Mercato Ritrovato: This is a flea market held every Sunday at Bologna's old brewery. It's a terrific spot to look for antiques, collectibles, and other one-of-a-kind stuff.

Artigiano in Fiera: This is an annual trade expo held in Bologna. It's a terrific site to discover handcrafted items from throughout Italy.

Bottega Verde: This is a shop chain that provides natural cosmetics and home goods. They provide a diverse range of items at competitive prices.

Here are some tips for getting hands-on experience at Bologna's markets and artisan shops:

Bargain: Bargaining is typical in several marketplaces, so don't be scared to haggle.

Prepare to walk: Because the markets are in the ancient core of Bologna, you should be prepared to stroll.

Bring some cash: Credit cards are not accepted at all markets.

Have fun with it: Shopping at local markets and artisan stores in Bologna is a terrific opportunity to learn about the city's culture and history.

Here are some more helpful hints for arranging a shopping trip to Bologna:

- The ideal time to shop in Bologna is during the week when the markets are less congested.
- There are several shopping trips available, so choose one that matches your interests and budget.
- If you are on a tight budget, the Quadrilatero area has numerous hidden beauties.
- If you want a more luxurious shopping experience, travel to the Via

Indipendenza neighborhood

Fashion and Design Boutiques

Bologna is an Italian city famed for its fashion and design in the Emilia-Romagna area. There are many independent shops and design businesses in the city where you may discover unique and fashionable apparel, accessories, and home items.

Here are some of Bologna's most popular fashion and design boutiques:

Collezioni Privata: This store has a carefully chosen collection of emerging designer women's clothes and accessories.

Luisa Spagnoli (Italy): This is a well-known Italian fashion label that provides a wide range of women's clothes, accessories, and home items.

Marni: This is a high-end fashion label noted for its unique designs.

Bottega Veneta: This is yet another high-end fashion label recognized for its high-quality leather items.

10 Corso Como: This is a multi-brand shop that carries a wide range of international fashion and design labels.

Here are some tips for getting hands-on experience at Bologna's fashion and design boutiques:

Be prepared to spend money: Bologna is a fashion city, so clothing and accessories will be expensive.

Do your Research: Before you go shopping, do some study on the many shops in Bologna. This will help you limit your options and save time.

Be willing to try new things: Bologna is an excellent location for discovering new fashion trends. Don't be frightened to attempt new things.

Have fun with it: Shopping at Bologna's fashion and design stores is an excellent opportunity to learn about the city's culture and fashion.

Here are some more helpful hints for arranging a shopping trip to Bologna:

- The ideal time to shop in Bologna is during the week when the boutiques are less crowded.
- There are several shopping trips available, so choose one that matches your interests and budget.
- If you are on a tight budget, the Quadrilatero area has numerous hidden beauties.
- If you want a more luxurious shopping experience, travel to the Via Indipendenza neighborhood.

Souvenirs to Bring Home

Here are some of the greatest Bologna souvenirs to buy:

Tortellini: Tortellini are a kind of pasta native to Bologna. It is created with fresh pasta dough and filled with either meat or cheese. Tortellini may be purchased in a variety of forms, including fresh, dried, and frozen.

Balsamic vinegar: This is a kind of vinegar created from grapes harvested in Italy's Modena area. It has been aged for many years, and the longer it has been aged, the more costly it has gotten. Balsamic vinegar goes well with salads, meats, and cheeses.

Modenese mustard: This is a sort of mustard created using wine, vinegar, and spices. It is a favorite condiment in Bologna, and it also makes an excellent keepsake.

Parmigiano-Reggiano cheese: This is a kind of hard cheese manufactured from cow's milk. It is matured for at least 12 months, and the longer it is aged, the higher the price. Parmigiano-Reggiano cheese goes well with pasta, salads, and sandwiches.

Handmade ceramics: Handmade ceramics are well-known in Bologna. There are several things available, including bowls, plates, and figurines.

Here are some suggestions for purchasing souvenirs in Bologna:

- Do your research: Before you start shopping, do some research on the many souvenirs available in Bologna. This will help you limit your options and save time.
- Be prepared to bargain: Bargaining is typical in certain of Bologna's marketplaces. Don't be scared to bargain to obtain the best deal.
- Buy from local companies, Try to buy souvenirs from local shops wherever feasible. This will benefit the local economy.
- Pack carefully: Make sure to pack your keepsakes carefully so they don't break or get damaged on your trip.

Entertainment and Nightlife

D iscover Bologna's dynamic entertainment and nightlife with a kaleidoscope of cultural offers that suit the interests of every visitor. Visit the city's quaint theaters to immerse yourself in its vibrant creative tapestry, where live plays come to life onstage, telling heartfelt tales that speak to the spirit. Bologna's many music venues and performances guarantee a symphony of experiences for music lovers, ranging from small jazz bars to large concert halls.

Bologna's intriguing nightlife scene emerges when the sun sets, a monument to its vibrant personality. Wander through the bustling streets and discover an array of bars and pubs, each with its own unique atmosphere, offering everything from classic cocktails to local brews. At night, the city really comes to life, beckoning you to take part in its vibrancy and create lifelong memories.

Beyond the specific locations, Bologna's calendar is packed with cultural activities and celebrations that encapsulate the city's history. There is always an event to fascinate and inspire, from traditional events that honor long-standing customs to cutting-edge creative displays. Bologna's entertainment and nightlife provide an exciting voyage into the heart of Italian culture and joie de vivre, whether you're a seasoned tourist or just starting out.

Theaters and Live Performances

There are theaters and performance places all across the city, with events ranging from opera and ballet to theater and comedy.

For visitors, these are some of the top theaters in Bologna:

Teatro Comunale di Bologna is the city's principal opera theatre and produces a broad range of productions throughout the year. Tickets might be pricey, but the experience is well worth it.

Teatro Arena del Sole is a little theater that hosts a range of acts such as theater, dance, and music. Tickets are less expensive than at the Teatro Comunale.

Il Celebrazioni Theatre is a contemporary theater that showcases a wide range of contemporary acts such as theater, dance, and music. Ticket prices are generally lower than at the Teatro Comunale or Teatro Arena del Sole.

Teatro Duse is a historic theater that accommodates a wide range of acts, such as theater, dance, and music. Ticket prices are generally lower than at the Teatro Comunale or Teatro Arena del Sole.

Teatro Testoni Ragazzi is a children's and young people's theater. It features a wide range of acts, such as theater, dance, and music. Tickets are generally quite cheap.

In addition to these theaters, Bologna has a plethora of additional performing venues, including:

- Manzoni Auditorium is a huge concert venue that presents a range of musical acts.
- Estragon Club is a jazz club where live music is performed.
- Covo Club is a rock club where live music is performed.

- The Teatro Anatomico is a historic theater that today hosts concerts and other events.
- Salaborsa is a cultural center that organizes activities such as theater, dance, and music.

The cost of tickets for live performances in Bologna varies according to the venue and the event.

Ticket prices for opera and ballet events at the Teatro Comunale range from €50 to €200. Ticket prices for theatrical and comedy acts at the Teatro Arena del Sole range from €15 to €50. Tickets for smaller theaters and performing places are often even more inexpensive.

Check the websites of the different theaters and performance locations to learn about upcoming live performances in Bologna. The Bologna Welcome website also offers information about forthcoming events.

Here are several suggestions for seeing live concerts in Bologna:

- Purchase your tickets in advance, particularly if you want to watch a production at the Teatro Comunale.
- To prevent crowds, arrive early.
- Dress properly for the performance.
- Be considerate to the other audience members.
- Have fun watching the program!

Music Venues and Concerts

Bologna has a thriving music culture, and there are several locations to select from, depending on your musical preferences. Here are a handful of Bologna's greatest music venues:

The city's principal opera venue, the Teatro Comunale di Bologna, also presents a range of other events, including classical music, jazz, and world music. Tickets are pricey, but the acoustics are superb, and the ambiance is simply amazing.

Estragon is a jazz club that has been showcasing live music for over 30 years. With a capacity of approximately 200 people, it is a tiny and intimate venue. Tickets are often inexpensive, and the atmosphere is always calm and welcoming.

The Covo Club is a rock club that has been in operation since the 1970s. With a capacity of approximately 1,000 persons, it is a bigger arena than Estragon. Ticket prices are often higher than at Estragon, but the club is recognized for its rowdy and dynamic environment.

Link Bologna is an underground cultural institution that organizes music events such as electronic music, techno, and house. It's a favorite hangout for young people, and the vibe is usually upbeat and energetic.

Muratella is a summer event held in a park on Bologna's outskirts. It features a wide range of musical styles, including rock, pop, and indie. The event is a terrific chance to spend time outside while also seeing some of your favorite acts.

Concert ticket costs in Bologna vary based on the venue and the act. Concert tickets at the Teatro Comunale may be costly, ranging from €50 to €200. Tickets for smaller venues, such as Estragon and Covo Club, are often less expensive, ranging from €15 to €50. Muratella festival tickets are generally approximately €20.

Here are some tips for going to concerts in Bologna:

Purchase your tickets in advance, particularly if you want to see a major musician at the Teatro Comunale.

- To prevent crowds, arrive early.
- Dress in weather-appropriate attire.
- Be considerate of the other concertgoers.
- Have a good time!

Bologna's Thriving Nightlife Scene

With a strong underground culture and a vibrant student population, Bologna's nightlife scene has something for everyone.

Bologna's nightlife revolves around the University District. This is the place to go for the cheapest beers and the liveliest atmosphere. The streets around Via Zamboni and Via delle Belle Arti are densely packed with pubs and clubs catering to a youthful audience.

Head to the Historic Center if you want something a bit more refined. A broader selection of pubs and clubs catering to a more older population may be found here. There are also a lot of rooftop bars with spectacular city views.

Whatever you're searching for, you'll find it in Bologna's nightlife scene.

Here are a handful of the greatest venues in Bologna to party:

The Freakout Club is a famous club for fans of electronic music. The club offers a huge dance floor as well as a cutting-edge sound system.

Numa Club is another prominent electronic music club. The club has a warehouse-style ambiance and is situated in an industrial region outside of the city core.

Cluricaune Irish Pub is an excellent choice for a drink and live music. The bar has a classic Irish feel and is popular with locals and visitors alike.

Hops & Grains is a craft beer pub that serves a broad variety of beers on tap. You may also have a bite to eat before or after your beverages from the bar's tiny food menu.

Every night of the week, La Cantina Bentivoglio presents live music performances. The club is housed in a magnificent, ancient basement and is an excellent venue for live music and tasty cuisine.

Bologna's nightlife scene has relatively inexpensive costs. A drink in a pub will cost you roughly €5–10, while a club ticket will cost you around €15–20.

Here are some suggestions for having a good time in Bologna's nightlife:

- Arrive early. The top pubs and clubs tend to fill up fast, so get there early to escape the lines.
- Make an effort to look your best. Bologna's nightlife scene is highly trendy, thus dressing up is recommended.
- Be ready to dance. Bologna is a city that likes to dance, so be ready to get down!
- Have a good time! The nightlife in Bologna is all about having fun, so relax, let loose, and have a good time.

Bars and Pubs for Every Taste

With a solid underground culture and a vibrant student population, Bologna's nightlife scene has something for everyone.

Bologna's nightlife revolves around the University District. This is the place to go for the cheapest beers and the liveliest atmosphere. The streets around Via Zamboni and Via delle Belle Arti are densely packed with pubs and clubs catering to a youthful audience.

Head to the Historic Center if you want something a bit more refined. A broader selection of pubs and clubs catering to a more older population may be found here. There are also a lot of rooftop bars with spectacular city views.

Whatever you're searching for, you'll find it in Bologna's nightlife scene.

Here are a handful of the greatest venues in Bologna to party:

The Freakout Club is a famous club for fans of electronic music. The club offers a huge dance floor as well as a cutting-edge sound system.

Numa Club is another prominent electronic music club. The club has a warehouse-style ambiance and is situated in an industrial region outside of the city core.

Cluricaune Irish Pub is an excellent choice for a drink and live music. The bar has a classic Irish feel and is popular with locals and visitors alike.

Hops & Grains is a craft beer pub that serves a broad variety of beers on tap. You may also have a bite to eat before or after your beverages from the bar's tiny food menu.

Every night of the week, La Cantina Bentivoglio presents live music performances. The club is housed in a magnificent, ancient basement and is an excellent venue for live music and tasty cuisine.

Bologna's nightlife scene has relatively inexpensive costs. A drink in a pub will cost you roughly €5–10, while a club ticket will cost you around €15–20.

Here are some suggestions for having a good time in Bologna's nightlife:

- Arrive early. The top pubs and clubs tend to fill up fast, so get there early to escape the lines.
- Make an effort to look your best. Bologna's nightlife scene is highly trendy,

thus dressing up is recommended.

- Be ready to dance. Bologna is a city that likes to dance, so be ready to get down!
- Have a good time! The nightlife in Bologna is all about having fun, so relax, let loose, and have a good time.

Cultural Events and Festivals

There are always a variety of events and festivals going on, ranging from traditional to modern. Here are a few of Bologna's greatest cultural events and festivals:

Bologna Festival of Contemporary Arts (Bè Bologna Estate)

Bè Bologna Estate is an event that encompasses music, theater, and cinema. It is held every summer from May through September and includes a variety of activities ranging from small concerts to large exhibits.

Most events are free, although some may have a minor entry charge..

Highlights: The festival offers a diverse choice of activities, ensuring that there is something for everyone. Outdoor concerts, film screenings, and art installations are among the attractions.

Il Cinema Ritrovato

Il Cinema Ritrovato is a film festival dedicated to the rediscovery of classic cinema. Every year, in July, the festival showcases a collection of great and rare films from across the globe.

Ticket prices begin at €8.

Highlights: The festival presents a diverse selection of films, ranging from silent masterpieces to current arthouse cinema. It's a fantastic chance to view films that you would not otherwise be able to see.

Danza Urbana

Danza Urbana is an event that celebrates urban dancing. Every year in August, the event showcases a range of dance acts ranging from street dance to hip hop.

Tickets start at €10 and go up from there.

Highlights: The festival offers a diverse spectrum of dance acts, ensuring that there is something for everyone. Breakdancing contests and capoeira demonstrations are among the attractions.

Bologna Carnevale (Bologna Carnival)

Carnevale di Bologna is a traditional carnival held in February. The carnival includes a number of activities, ranging from masked balls to street parades.

Most events are free, although some may have a minor entry charge.

Highlights: There are a variety of activities during the carnival, so there is something for everyone. The masked parties, street parades, and food vendors are among the attractions.

Other celebrations and events

In addition to these big festivals, Bologna hosts several cultural events and festivals throughout the year. Here are some more examples:

Il Festival del Fumetto (Comics Festival): Every spring, in April, this festival comprises a range of comic-related activities, including exhibits, seminars, and screenings.

Il Festival del Cinema Indipendente: This festival takes place every year, in October, and showcases a selection of independent films from throughout the globe.

The Festival della Musica Antica (Early Music Festival): is held every year in July and comprises a variety of early music performances ranging from the Middle Ages through the Baroque era.

Il Festivaletteratura (Literary Festival): This festival takes place every September in the autumn and includes a range of literary activities such as readings, seminars, and discussions.

Bologna cultural events and festivals: What to Expect

- Purchase your tickets early: Because many events and festivals sell out fast, purchasing your tickets in advance is a smart idea.
- Examine the timetable: Check the event calendar before you attend to ensure you don't miss anything.
- Dress appropriately: Some events have a dress code, so dress accordingly.
- Be patient: Some events may have large lines, so be patient and prepared to wait.
- Have a good time! Cultural events and festivals are a terrific opportunity to learn about Bologna's culture, so have fun and enjoy yourself!

Practical Information

Navigating a new city like Bologna may be a thrilling experience, but having important practical information at your fingertips is key for a seamless voyage. In terms of language and communication, Italian is the most widely spoken language in Bologna. While English may be understood in tourist areas, it's a good idea to have a basic Italian phrasebook or translation software with you to improve interactions with locals.

It is vital to understand the currency and banking systems. The Euro (€) is the currency in use, and ATMs are easily accessible for cash withdrawals. Inform your bank of your trip dates to avoid problems with card use.

Prioritizing safety is essential. Bologna is quite secure, although, as with any city, be wary of pickpocketing in busy places. Keep an eye on your stuff and avoid publicly exhibiting valuables.

It is critical to maintain excellent health and medical procedures. The city's medical services are outstanding, with pharmacies designated with a green cross. It's a good idea to obtain travel insurance that covers medical expenditures, giving you peace of mind during your travels.

Positive encounters are fostered by understanding local customs and etiquette. Italians place a high priority on politeness and decency. A handshake or a brief kiss on both cheeks is usual when welcoming. Dining etiquette involves waiting for the host to begin the meal and correctly utilizing utensils.

Language and Communication

Language

Bologna is a city in Italy, and Italian is the official language. However, a few additional languages are spoken in the city, notably Emilian, an Italian regional dialect, and English.

Italian

Italian is a Romance language spoken by about 60 million people throughout the globe. Italy, San Marino, Vatican City, and Switzerland all speak it as their official language. Many other nations, like Argentina, Brazil, and Canada, speak Italian as well.

Italian is a very simple language to learn, particularly for those who know other Romance languages. The grammar is straightforward, and the pronunciation is consistent. However, English speakers may encounter a few difficulties while learning Italian. One difficulty is pronouncing specific consonants, for as the "c" in "ciao" and the "g" in "gelato". Another difficulty is using gendered nouns and adjectives.

Emilian

Emilian is an Italian regional dialect spoken in the Emilia-Romagna area of Italy. It is closely related to Italian, although there are minor phonetic and lexical distinctions. Emilian is not an official language in the area, although it is widely spoken.

English

English is growing more popular in Bologna, and it is not unusual to hear individuals conversing in the language. This is because Bologna is a major tourist destination with numerous companies and organizations catering to English-speaking guests.

Communication in Bologna

The locals will appreciate your ability to communicate in Italian. Don't be concerned if you don't speak Italian fluently. Many people in Bologna speak English, so you'll be OK with just that.

If you're having trouble communicating in Italian, consider using basic words and phrases. Slang and colloquialisms should be avoided.

If you don't comprehend anything, be patient and don't get irritated. Your attempts to converse in their language would be appreciated by the people.

If you're lost or in need of assistance, don't hesitate to ask for instructions. Most people in Bologna will gladly assist you.

Here are some useful communication strategies for Bologna:

- Before you leave, learn some fundamental Italian phrases. This will assist you in getting by in ordinary circumstances.

- Install a translation app on your smartphone. If you need to translate a word or phrase, this might be useful.
- Prepare to make hand movements. Italians are extremely expressive people who often communicate using hand gestures.
- Make no apologies for making blunders. When learning a new language, everyone makes mistakes.
- Simply relax and enjoy yourself! Communicating with locals is an excellent method to learn about the culture and meet new people.

Basic Italian Phrases

Introductions and greetings:

- Ciao (informal) – Hello
- Buongiorno? (formal) – Hello and good morning.
- Buon pomeriggio. – Hello and good day.
- Buona sera (evening? (evening) – Hello and good evening.
- Arrivederci (farewell)
- Per favore(per favore)
- Grazie (thank you).
- (Prego) You're welcome
- Mi dispiace (sorry)
- Come sta? (How are you doing?)
- Sto bene, grazie. E tu? (I'm fine, thank you. And you?)
- Mi chiamo (my name is [your name].)
- Piacere di conoscerti (It's a pleasure to finally meet you.)

Directions:

- Dove sono i bagni? (Where are the restrooms?)
- Dove posso trovare un taxi? (Where can I find a taxi?)
- Come si va alla stazione? (Could you please advise me how to go to the train station?)

- Quanto costa un biglietto per il centro? (What is the price of a ticket to the city center?)
- Scusi, mi pu? indicare la strada per...? (Excuse me, can you tell me the way to...?)
- Sono in Piazza Navona. (I'm in Piazza Navona.)
- Devo andare a sinistra o a destra? (Do I go left or right?)
- lontano? (Is it far?)

Accommodation:

- Vorrei una camera. (I would like a room.)
- A che prezzo? (How much does it cost?)
- C'? un bagno privato? (Is there a private bathroom?)
- C'? la televisione? (Is there a TV?)
- C'? l'aria condizionata? (Is there air conditioning?)
- Posso vedere la camera? (Can I see the room?)
- Prendo la camera. (I'll take the room.)

Food and drink:

- Vorrei un menu, per favore. (I would like a menu, please.)
- Cosa mi consiglia? (What do you recommend?)
- Ho fame. (I'm hungry.)
- Sono pieno. (I'm full.)
- Il conto, per favore. (The bill, please.)
- Buon appetito! (Enjoy your meal!)
- Grazie per la cena. (Thank you for dinner.)
- Il vino? buono. (The wine is good.)
- Il caff forte. (The coffee is strong.)

Shopping:

- Quanto costa? (How much does it cost?)

- Lo posso provare? (Can I try it on?)
- Mi fa un sacchetto? (Can I have a bag?)
- Vorrei pagare con la carta di credito. (I'd rather pay with a credit card.)
- Non ho il resto. (I don't have change.)
- Grazie per l'acquisto. (Thank you for your purchase.)

Emergency:

- Aiuto! (Help!)
- Aiuto! (Help!)
- Chiamo la polizia! (I'm calling the police!)
- Sto male. (I'm not feeling well.)
- Ho bisogno di un dottore. (I need a doctor.)
- Sono stato derubato. (I've been robbed.)
- Ho perso i miei documenti. (I've lost my documents.)

Currency and Banking

The euro (EUR) is the currency in use in Bologna. The euro is the official currency of the 19 member countries of the European Union. It is split into 100 cents.

Banks and ATMs

In Bologna, there are several banks and ATMs. Major credit and debit cards are accepted at the majority of banks and ATMs. It is, however, always a good idea to verify with your bank before traveling to ensure that your card will be accepted.

Currency exchange

Banks, exchange bureaus, and certain hotels provide currency exchange services. The exchange rate may differ from one location to the next, so it is a good idea to shop around.

Traveler's checks

Traveler's checks are no longer as readily recognized as they once were. You may be able to trade them in banks and exchange bureaus, though.

Tips for using currency in Bologna

- When you arrive in Bologna, it is a good idea to have some euros on hand. This will help you to cover small costs such as cabs and groceries.
- You may also withdraw euros from ATMs using your credit or debit card. However, there may be a fee if you use your card outside of the United States.
- Keep careful track of your purchases to avoid overdrawing your account.
- If you need to convert money, make sure you obtain a decent rate.
- Traveler's checks may also be utilized, although they are not as generally recognized as they formerly were.

Here are some helpful hints when exchanging money in Bologna:

- Inquire with your bank about the best manner to convert currencies.
- Before you switch money, check the exchange rate.
- Keep careful track of your expenditures.
- Use a credit or debit card with no international transaction fees.
- Keep some euros on hand for minor costs.
- If you want assistance, do not be hesitant to ask for it

Practical Tips and Safety

Safety Tips for Travelers

- Always be aware of your surroundings. This is especially important in congested areas and tourist areas, where pickpocketing is more prevalent.
- Keep your belongings close at hand and avoid carrying large sums of money.
- Don't flaunt costly items, Jewelry, electronics, and even your smartphone fall into this category. Thieves prefer to target people who are perceived to be wealthy or flashy.
- Be cautious at night: While Bologna is generally safe at night, it's always a good idea to be cautious. Avoid walking alone in areas that are dark or deserted.
- Instead of walking long distances, take public transportation or a taxi.
- This will prevent you from becoming disoriented or being targeted by criminals.
- Keep hydrated and limit your alcohol consumption. Alcohol can impair your judgment and make you more likely to commit a crime.
- Believe your instincts. Don't be afraid to leave if you feel unsafe in a situation. It is always better to be safe than sorry.
- Keep in touch with friends and family back home. Inform them of your travel plans and keep in touch with them regularly.
- Keep a copy of your passport and other important documents with you at all times. This will come in handy if you misplace your passport or other

valuables.

- Learn some fundamental Italian phrases. This will allow you to communicate with locals and ask for assistance if necessary.
- Understand the local customs and culture. This will assist you in avoiding any mistakes that could put you in danger.
- Any incidents should be reported to the police as soon as possible. This will assist them in locating criminals and preventing future crimes.

ere are some tips that you might find useful:

- Keep your bag closed and close to you.
- Do not, under any circumstances, leave your bag on the ground.
- Keep an eye out for people who are following you.
- If you believe you are being followed, seek refuge in a crowded area or at a police station.
- Don't accept rides from strangers.
- Only use ATMs that are in well-lit, busy areas.
- When using your credit or debit card, exercise caution. Keep an eye on your card at all times and immediately report any suspicious activity to your bank.

Health and Medical Services

The Italian healthcare system is universal, meaning that all citizens and legal residents have access to free or low-cost healthcare. As a tourist, however, you may not be eligible for the same benefits. It is critical to purchase travel insurance before traveling to Bologna to cover medical expenses.

If you require medical attention while in Bologna, go to the nearest hospital or clinic. You can also dial 118 to summon an ambulance.

The following are the main hospitals in Bologna:

- **Policlinico Sant'Orsola-Malpighi**: This is Bologna's largest hospital, and it provides a wide range of medical services.
- **Ospedale Maggiore:** This is another large hospital in Bologna that also serves as a teaching facility.
- **Ospedale Villa Saliceto**: This is a private hospital that provides a wide range of medical services, including cosmetic surgery.

Here are some more suggestions for staying healthy in Bologna:

- Drink plenty of water.
- Maintain a healthy diet.
- Get enough rest.
- Hands should be washed frequently.

- Avoid coming into contact with sick people.
- Obtain vaccinations for common diseases such as measles, mumps, and rubella.

Local Customs and Etiquette

Greetings: It is customary in Bologna to shake hands when greeting someone. It is also polite to introduce yourself if you are meeting someone for the first time. Because Italians are generally friendly and warm, don't be afraid to smile and make eye contact.

Dress code: There is no strict dress code in Bologna, but modest clothing is generally considered polite. This includes not wearing shorts, tank tops, or other revealing clothing. When visiting a church or other religious site, you should dress even more conservatively.

Tipping is not expected in Bologna, but it is greatly appreciated. If you are pleased with the service, you may leave a small tip of around 10%.

Public transportation is an excellent way to get around in Bologna. The city has an extensive bus and tram system, as well as a metro system.

Tickets can be purchased at newsstands and tobacco shops.

Taxis: Taxis are available in Bologna, but they are not cheap. Taxis are usually best for short distances or late at night.

Restaurants: It is customary to order aperitivi (appetizers) before your meal at a restaurant in Bologna. Small plates of food, such as cured meats, cheeses, or vegetables, are typically served. Pasta or pizza is usually served as the main course, followed by dessert.

Coffee is an important part of Italian culture, and Bologna is no exception. There are cafes all over the city, and people frequently stop for a coffee or espresso throughout the day.

Smoking is prohibited in the majority of public places in Bologna, including restaurants, bars, and cafes. There are a few designated smoking areas, but they are becoming less common.

Politeness: Italians are generally very polite people, but it is important to understand local customs and etiquette. Here are a few things to keep in mind:

- Say "please" and "thank you" often.
- Be considerate of other people's personal space.
- Make no noise or cause a commotion.
- Be aware of your body language.

Conclusion

Y ou've explored the mysteries of the city's famous buildings, roamed through quaint cobblestone streets, and savored the incomparable aromas of its world-renowned food as you've read through the pages of this travel book. The harmonic mix of old and contemporary, tradition and innovation, produces a compelling and appealing environment.

But Bologna is more than simply a destination; it's an experience that stays with you long after you've left. Whether you're a history buff, a foodie, an art aficionado, or just an adventurer at heart, Bologna has something for everyone.

As you say goodbye to this enthralling city, may the memories you've made here encourage your spirit of exploration and curiosity. Remember the warmth of the villagers' welcomes, the flavor of traditional pasta meals, and the incredible tales that each cobblestone corner tells. Your trip to Bologna is more than simply a travelogue chapter; it's a timeless story that you'll take with you wherever you go.

We hope that you will start on future trips with the same passion and open-mindedness that Bologna has instilled in you, with a heart full of treasured memories and a mind sparked by discovered knowledge. As the sun sets on your Bologna experience, may the light rise on a plethora of new adventures, each as rich and gratifying as the last. Safe travels, and may the spirit of Bologna guide you on every step of your extraordinary adventure.

Printed in Great Britain
by Amazon

42471749R10066